Dr. Michael Leach
and Dr. Meriel Lland

The World of Plants

illustrated by
Juanita Londoño-Gaviria

ARCTURUS

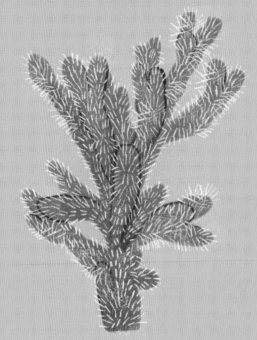

ARCTURUS

This edition published in 2022 by Arcturus Publishing Limited
26/27 Bickels Yard, 151–153 Bermondsey Street,
London SE1 3HA

Authors: Dr. Michael Leach and Dr. Meriel Lland
Illustrator: Juanita Londoño-Gaviria
Designer: Suzanne Cooper
Editor: Donna Gregory
Design Manager: Jessica Holliland
Editorial Manager: Joe Harris

ISBN: 978-1-3988-2015-9
CH008294NT
Supplier 42, Date 0922, PI 00002285

Printed in Singapore

CONTENTS

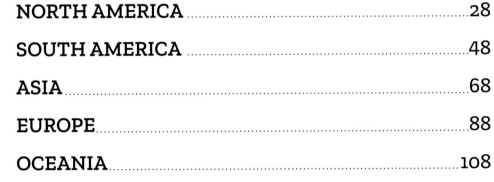

PAGES

PLANT PLANET

Life on Earth depends on plants; without them, we could not be here. They transform the Sun's energy, water, and carbon dioxide into the air we breathe and the food we eat. Plants can be as tall as buildings or so tiny they can only be spotted with a microscope. There are plants that live for many thousands of years and those that live for only a few weeks.

Plants work hard to feed and to reproduce. They communicate with animals and other plants to survive. They are skilled in disguise and have lots of tricks to help them avoid being eaten and to set seed. There are even some plants that eat animals!

NORTH AMERICA

SOUTH AMERICA

HABITATS: A PLACE TO CALL HOME

A habitat is an environment that plants and animals live in; somewhere they can find food and suitable growing conditions and reproduce. Wild plants help create habitats. They are influenced by weather, temperature, and the position of the continents on the Earth's surface. There are six major habitat types—freshwater, sea, forest, desert, grassland, and tundra.

SEA

FOREST

GRASSLAND

TUNDRA

DESERT

FRESHWATER

EUROPE

ASIA

AFRICA

OCEANIA

HOW IT ALL BEGAN: PANGEA

The Earth has not always looked like it does today. Millions of years ago, most of the land on the planet was joined together in one massive area called Pangea. Pangea lasted for about 100 million years and eventually fragmented. Chunks of land that we call continents changed position, driven by powerful movements in the Earth's surface. The continents are still moving. As you read this book, Europe and North America are steadily shifting farther apart by about 2.5 cm (1 in) every year.

SEVEN CONTINENTS

Most of the Earth's land lies in seven continents—Africa, Europe, North America, South America, Asia, Antarctica, and Oceania. Oceania covers the continent of Australia, along with the 25,000 islands of the Pacific.

WHAT IS A PLANT?

Plants are living organisms. Most contain a green pigment called chlorophyll. This chemical takes the energy of sunlight and carbon dioxide from the air and transforms them into a food called glucose. This process is called photosynthesis and it releases oxygen, which all animals need to breathe.

Leaves are where photosynthesis takes place. At night, when there is no light, plants stop photosynthesizing and respire instead—a process where plants take in oxygen and release carbon dioxide.

THE KINGDOM OF PLANTS

Botanists—scientists who study plants—tell us that there are about 400,000 different types of plant on Earth. More species are discovered all the time. The first land plants, including mosses and ferns, evolved around 470 million years ago. They slowly changed into the vast range we see today—from buttercups and bananas to giant redwood trees.

To bring a little order to this variety, botanists divide plants into nonflowering and flowering plants. Within these groups, there are many different species. Flowering plants make up more than 90 percent of all plants.

Ancient plants

Horsetails first appeared around 200 million years ago, in the time of the dinosaurs. They still thrive in most parts of the world, except Australasia.

PLANT REPRODUCTION

Plants reproduce in two ways: sexually and asexually.

Sexual reproduction requires that plants have flowers and produce seeds. First, pollen is carried by the wind or by insects from one flower to another. When pollen reaches the new flower, it travels to the ovary and fertilizes the egg cells. This produces seeds. The seeds are dispersed by the wind or insects. Some seeds will go on to make new plants that are similar but not identical to the parents.

Asexual reproduction is also called cloning. This method allows plants to form new plants all by themselves! Most gardeners grow—or clone—potatoes from other small potatoes. A clone can grow from the roots, stems, leaves, or flowers of the parent plant. It is always identical to the parent plant. Cloning leads to faster plant life cycles but, because all offspring are identical, all are vulnerable to the same diseases or changes in environment.

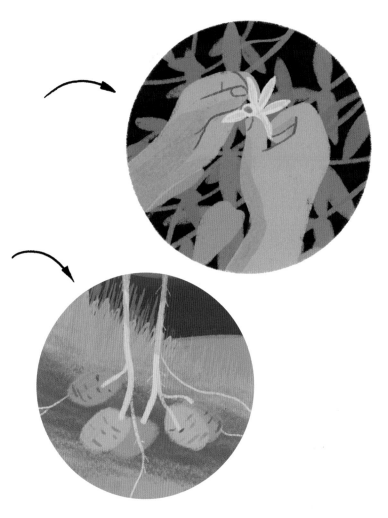

FUNGI AND THE WOOD WIDE WEB

Fungi are fantastic! Although not plants, their relationship with them is very special. They help to break down plant material to release nutrients for other species to take up, and their own network of fine roots—mycelia—merges with other species, such as trees, to help them communicate and share food! It's a little like the way the worldwide web helps people share information. The Wood Wide Web is simply amazing!

AFRICA

Africa is the world's second largest continent and the oldest. It contains 54 countries and the landscape is vast and varied. It is home to the Nile, the longest river, as well as to rift valleys, lakes, grassland, deserts, and tropical rain forests. Today, there are an estimated 45,000 plant species growing in Africa. The exact number is almost certainly higher as new species are being discovered constantly, particularly in the under-explored areas of forest in the Congo.

The richest diversity of African plants is found in rain forests. This habitat is warm and wet year round, allowing plants to photosynthesize and grow without the need to slow down in winter. Life is much harder for plants in the Sahel and other dry areas, such as the Moroccan Desert, which receive very little rain.

1 EGYPT: NILE DELTA

The rich soils of the delta are excellent for growing crops, including cotton! Soft, white strands surround the seeds of the cotton plant. These can be spun into thread to make textiles.

2 NORTH AFRICA and MOROCCO: ARGAN

Tree-climbing goats help the argan tree to disperse its seed in their droppings. Argan oil is an ingredient used in cosmetics worldwide.

3 NORTH AFRICA: SAHEL

The Sahel is home to extraordinary plants that can soften rocks and others that can help treat snake bites!

4 WEST AFRICA: KOLA NUT

This amazing tree gives us musical instruments, wood for making canoes, and cola to drink!

Potato
(Solanum tuberosum)

Baobab tree
(Adansonia digitata)

Papyrus (Cyperus papyrus) and *woven papyrus*

Gum arabic tree
(Senegalia senegal)

Blue water lily (Nymphaea nouchali)

Desert rose
(Adenium obesum)

Argan
(Argania spinosa)

Kola nut
(Cola acuminata)

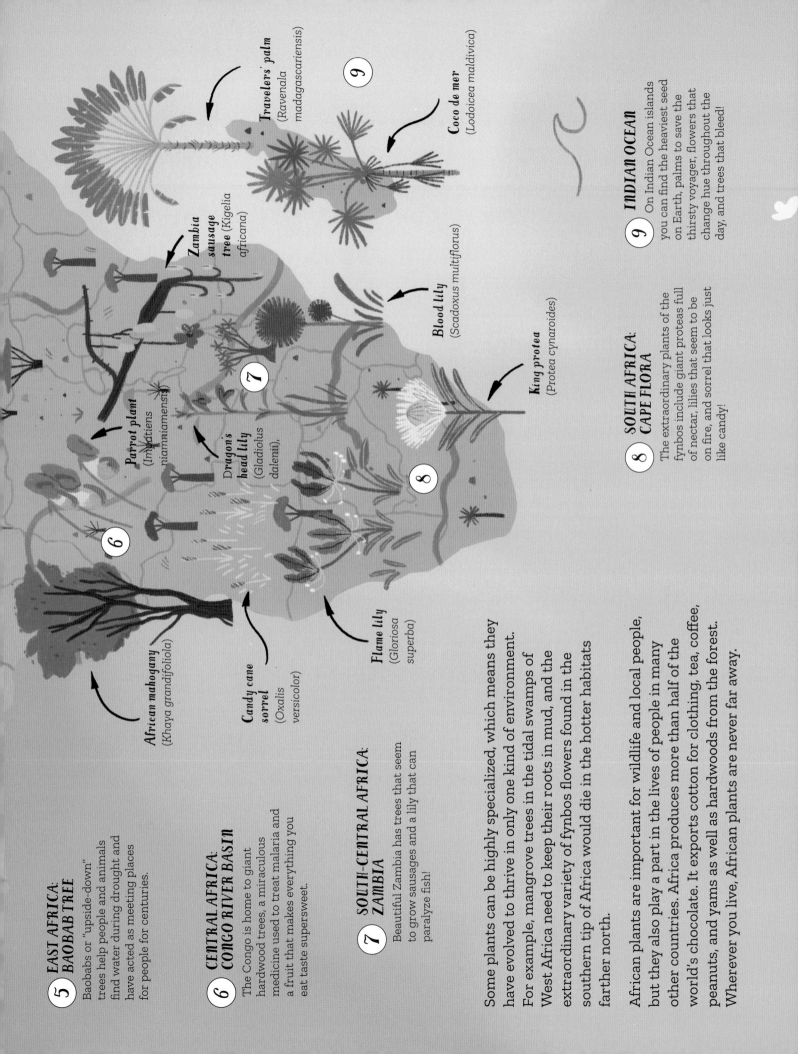

Travelers' palm
(*Ravenala madagascariensis*)

9

Coco de mer
(*Lodoicea maldivica*)

Zambia sausage tree (*Kigelia africana*)

Blood lily
(*Scadoxus multiflorus*)

7

King protea
(*Protea cynaroides*)

Parrot plant
(*Impatiens niamniamensis*)

Dragon's head lily
(*Gladiolus dalenii*),

6

8

African mahogany
(*Khaya grandifoliola*)

Candy cane sorrel
(*Oxalis versicolor*)

Flame lily
(*Gloriosa superba*)

9 **INDIAN OCEAN**
On Indian Ocean islands you can find the heaviest seed on Earth, palms to save the thirsty voyager, flowers that change hue throughout the day, and trees that bleed!

8 **SOUTH AFRICA: CAPE FLORA**
The extraordinary plants of the fynbos include giant proteas full of nectar, lilies that seem to be on fire, and sorrel that looks just like candy!

Some plants can be highly specialized, which means they have evolved to thrive in only one kind of environment. For example, mangrove trees in the tidal swamps of West Africa need to keep their roots in mud, and the extraordinary variety of fynbos flowers found in the southern tip of Africa would die in the hotter habitats farther north.

African plants are important for wildlife and local people, but they also play a part in the lives of people in many other countries. Africa produces more than half of the world's chocolate. It exports cotton for clothing, tea, coffee, peanuts, and yams as well as hardwoods from the forest. Wherever you live, African plants are never far away.

5 **EAST AFRICA: BAOBAB TREE**
Baobabs or "upside-down" trees help people and animals find water during drought and have acted as meeting places for people for centuries.

6 **CENTRAL AFRICA: CONGO RIVER BASIN**
The Congo is home to giant hardwood trees, a miraculous medicine used to treat malaria and a fruit that makes everything you eat taste supersweet.

7 **SOUTH-CENTRAL AFRICA: ZAMBIA**
Beautiful Zambia has trees that seem to grow sausages and a lily that can paralyze fish!

Sugarcane *(Saccharum officinarum)*
Sugarcane is a type of grass. It contains very high levels of sucrose, a natural sugar. When canes are crushed and boiled, they give us the sugar granules that we use to sweeten food.

Cotton *(Gossypium hirsutum)*
These plants were first discovered in Mexico but are now grown in many countries. The soft, white strands surrounding the seeds are spun into cloth. Egypt produces some of the world's most luxurious cotton.

Watermelon *(Citrullus lanatus)*
Watermelons are a versatile food and can be eaten raw, pickled, or added to stews, drunk as a juice, or made into wine. Watermelon seeds were found in the tomb of the Egyptian Pharaoh Tutankhamun.

Tiger nut *(Cyperus esculentus)*
Tiger nuts were one of the first agricultural crops sown by humans. Ripe nuts were gathered and dried.

Larkspur *(Consolida ajacis)*
The bright blue flowers contain a poison that can be deadly to humans and animals. Farmers are careful to remove these plants before cattle are allowed to graze in the delta.

Potato *(Solanum tuberosum)*
There are more than 5,000 different kinds of potatoes grown around the world. Potatoes are closely related to tomatoes and are one of Egypt's most important crops.

Plume thistle *(Cirsium rivulare)*
People living around the Nile Delta used to cook and eat the stems of thistles before more tasty crops were introduced.

NILE DELTA, EGYPT

The Nile is the longest river in Africa. It brings life to the dry, desert landscape of Egypt. Over thousands of years, the current has washed small amounts of soil from the riverbanks and carried it downstream toward the sea.

As the Nile starts to flow into the Mediterranean Sea, the river becomes slow and shallow. It splits into channels and widens out. This is the Nile wetland, or delta. It has rich, fertile soil and is ideal for growing crops such as potatoes and cotton. Egypt's year-round warm weather helps plants thrive here. They form a huge green oasis within the surrounding sandy desert that can be seen from space!

Today, the plants of this vital habitat are threatened by global warming. Rises in the sea level of the Mediterranean mean that salt water can flow into the delta and change the kinds of plants and crops that survive there.

Papyrus paper

Papyrus (Cyperus papyrus)
Papyrus reeds grow in shallow water. Around 5,000 years ago, Egyptians dried and flattened these reeds to make some of the world's first paper.

Celery (Apium graveolens)
Celery is a very thirsty crop and needs a constant supply of water.

Water lettuce (Pistia stratiotes)
Water lettuce traps air in its leaves to help it float on the surface of the water. It is known as "Nile cabbage" but is toxic if eaten raw.

Mediterranean Sea

Egypt

Sudan

Red Sea

Nile River

Blue water lily
(Nymphaea nouchali)
Water lily flowers open in mid-morning and close at sunset. Each flower only lasts for four days.

ARGAN FORESTS of NORTH AFRICA

Argan trees (*Argania spinosa*) have evolved to survive in the hot, dry semidesert of south-west Morocco. Their canopy of small, leathery leaves lose little water and their short, gnarled trunks are anchored by deep roots.

Trees are rare in this barren landscape and are treated with care because they bring many benefits. They provide food and medicine for humans and animals in the form of argan oil. Their roots bind the soil to stop it from being eroded by winds, and mature trees give shade against the hot sun.

Even when an argan tree dies, at around 200 years old, every part of it is recycled as timber or firewood. Nothing happens quickly in the argan forest; it takes 50 years for trees to produce fruit. Commercial overuse and deforestation threaten the trees and they are now protected as an endangered species.

Animal fodder

Argan leaves are excellent food for camels, sheep, and goats. They also eat the nut pulp once all the oil has been extracted.

Poop oil!

Clever local goats have learned to climb high into the argan trees to eat the fruits. Traditionally, the nuts found in goat droppings were gathered up, processed, and turned into oil.

Morocco

Argan forest

Beauty oil

Argan oil has become a popular antiaging beauty product in recent times. The fruit of the argan tree contains a nut, inside which is a kernel. The kernel is crushed and the pulp is then squeezed to extract the precious oil.

Spring bloomers

Argan flowers appear in early spring, ready to be pollinated by insects.

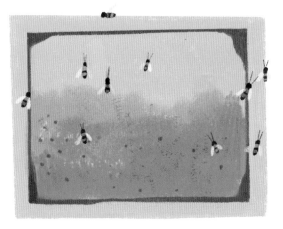

Busy bees

Argan flowers attract bees, so many farmers keep bee hives nearby. The bees gather nectar and the hives give a good supply of honey.

New generation

Farmers are careful not to take away all the seeds. A few of the best seeds are planted ready for the next generation of argan trees to grow.

Multipurpose oil

Argan oil, once known only to the local Berber tribes, is now widely used in cooking, for treating wounds, and in skincare, cosmetics, and perfume. The oil has a nutty taste.

THE SAHEL

The Sahel is a vast, dry or "semiarid" area south of the Sahara Desert and north of a band of rich, green forests and grassland. It spans ten countries and measures 5,900 km (3,670 mi) from west to east.

This is a region of extremes. The rains bring a spurt of growth; grass becomes lush and flowers bloom in the damp soil. As the temperatures soar and the land heats up, these plants fade away. Trees lose their leaves and there is little growing in the intense heat. Then, there are many months with no rain at all.

Only a small number of the most adaptable plants can survive all year round. These plants are important to the local people as few crops can be grown in this harsh landscape. Sahel plants provide food for humans and domestic animals. They are also used to treat wounds and produce goods that can be traded or sold.

Gum arabic tree
(Senegalia senegal)
The sap of gum arabic is used to thicken chewing gum.

Balsam spurge
(Euphorbia balsamifera)
The sticky sap of this balsam spurge is poisonous, but it produces a chemical that is used as a painkiller by local dentists.

Thyme
(Thymus vulgaris)
Thyme leaves have long been used as an antiseptic.

Red acacia *(Vachellia seyal)*
Acacia trees have very sharp 8 cm (3 in)-long spines on their branches. These weapons deter most animals from eating the acacia's leaves.

Desert rose
(Adenium obesum)

The desert rose stores water in its swollen stem. It grows wild in the Sahel and is a very popular houseplant throughout the world.

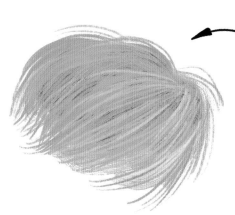

Lovegrass *(Eragrostis curvula)*

Most of a lovegrass plant is hidden underground. The grass can grow to 1.85 m (6 ft) tall but the root system can be 4 m (13 ft) deep and 3 m (9.8 ft) wide.

Dead Sea apple
(Calotropis procera)

Sap from the stem of Dead Sea apples can be used to treat the bites of some venomous snakes.

Pearl millet *(Cenchrus americanus)*

Pearl millet produces a seed that can be used to make excellent flatbreads.

Doum palm
(Hyphaene thebaica)

Doum palm trees are either female or male. There are flowers on every doum palm, but only female palms produce fruit.

Samwa
(Cleome droserifolia)

Samwa roots produce chemicals that make rocks become soft. This allows the plants to grow in areas with very little soil.

Hanza
(Boscia senegalensis)

Hanza is one of the few types of fruit tree that is able to grow in the Sahel.

Umbrella thorn *(Vachellia tortilis)*

Seeds of umbrella thorn trees are an important food for baboons.

KOLA NUT TREE, WEST AFRICA

People enjoy caffeine and archaeological evidence suggests we have been eating caffeine-packed kola nuts (*Cola nitida* and *Cola acuminata*) for centuries. They can be chewed raw, or roasted, crushed, and added to food or drinks. In the twentieth century, they became important in a range of manufactured drinks that were given the name "cola."

Tall, evergreen kola trees were once found growing naturally in West African rain forests but commercial crops are more widespread. They do not form fruits until they are four years old, but each one can produce up to 300 nuts (their seeds) every year. The bright red nuts grow inside fruits—or pods —that protect them from being eaten. The fruits are rough, mottled, and up to 20 cm (8 in) long. The nuts are harvested unripe because many forest animals eat the ripe seeds when the pods open naturally.

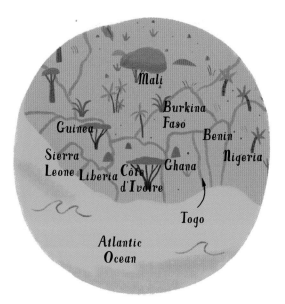

Leathery leaves

The kola nut tree somewhat resembles a chestnut (*Castanea*) tree. The leaves are long and ovoid in shape and have a leathery surface.

Tasty nuts

Kola nuts contain caffeine and are used in some chocolates and drinks.

Processing the pods

Once the pods are open, the seeds need to be dried before being used.

Shake, rattle, and roll

Musicians loosely tie dried kola nuts together with twine. When shaken, they make a sound just like maracas.

Pollination

Kola nut flowers are
pollinated by both the
wind and by insects.

Tasty seeds

Each pod holds up
to ten seeds. They
are a much-loved
food of birds, bats,
and squirrels.

Chimpanzees *(Pan troglodytes)*

Chimps are one of the few
animal species to use tools.
They use heavy stones to crack
open the hard kola pods and eat
the seeds inside.

Strong wood

The wood of kola nut trees is
strong and hard. They are often
used to make hollowed-out canoes.

A stable home

The baobab's branches make a perfect site for **red-billed buffalo weavers** (*Bubalornis niger*) to build their nests.

Just hanging out

Leopards (*Panthera pardus*) like to rest sitting high up, draped over a baobab branch.

Emergency rations

When there is nothing else to eat, **elephants** (*Loxodonta africana*) use their tusks to dig into baobabs to reach the damp wood inside.

Fruity conserve

Baobab fruit is bitter and tastes like lemon, but it makes an excellent preserve when it is simmered together with sugar.

Pendulous pods

Baobab fruit grows inside large egg-shaped pods that hang down from branches.

Versatile bark

Baobab bark is tough and hard-wearing. Long, thin strips can be taken off and woven into bags and hats. This does no harm to the tree as the bark grows back.

BAOBAB TREE, EAST AFRICA

The baobab tree (*Adansonia digitata*) is one of the world's longest living trees. The oldest was nearly 2,500 years of age. They are known as "upside-down trees" because their strange branches look exactly like the roots of a tree sticking up into the air.

Baobab flowers are pollinated by bats. They open at sunset, just before the bats leave their roosts. The flowers close before dusk to keep out of the sun. Baobabs can survive in very dry habitats because they can store water. During the wet season, baobab roots suck water from the ground and horde it inside their huge trunks. A single tree can hold 120,000 l (26,400 gallons, or the same amount of water as in 400 bathtubs), which will keep it alive when there is no rainfall. As baobabs get older, they don't grow taller. Instead, their trunks grow wider and can hold much more water.

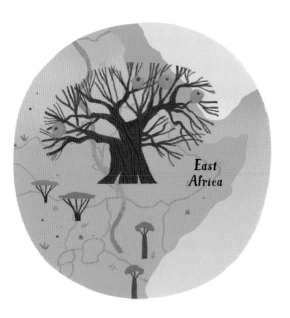

East Africa

Atlantic Ocean   Indian Ocean

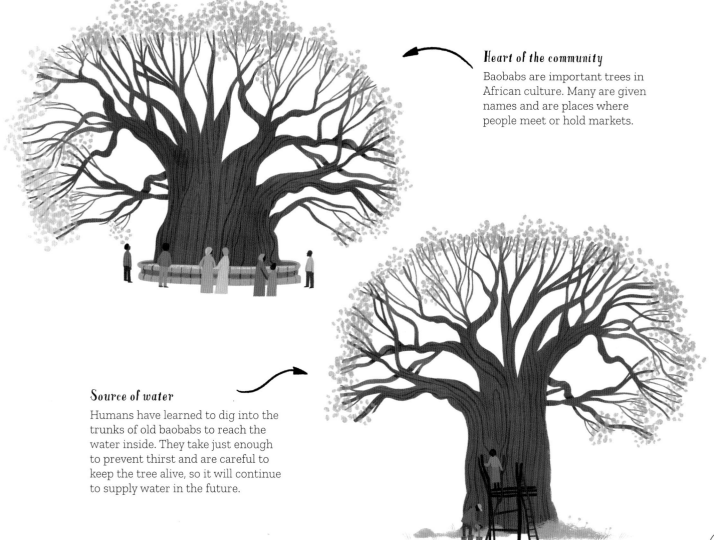

Heart of the community

Baobabs are important trees in African culture. Many are given names and are places where people meet or hold markets.

Source of water

Humans have learned to dig into the trunks of old baobabs to reach the water inside. They take just enough to prevent thirst and are careful to keep the tree alive, so it will continue to supply water in the future.

CONGO RIVER BASIN, SALONGA NATIONAL PARK

The Congo Basin contains the second-largest rain forest in the world. There are remote parts of this intricate equatorial forest that have not yet been properly explored or mapped. Every year, scientists discover new species of plants and animals.

Few people live in the forest and most make their home close to the giant Congo River. The small human population means that the Congo is not being destroyed as quickly as some rain forests, where people cut down trees for firewood, building materials, and timber to sell.

In open habitats, strong winds disperse seeds and carry them far from the parent plant. The Congo's isolated Salonga National Park is Africa's biggest forest reserve and accessible only by water. It is home to giant 50 m (160 ft)-high trees that slow any winds and prevent airborne seed dispersal. Instead, seeds are carried in animal droppings!

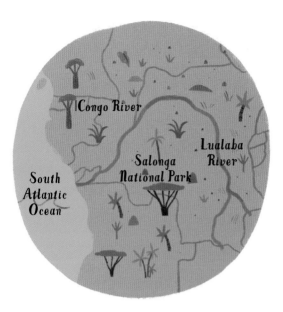

Sjambok pod
(Cassia abbreviata)
Sjambok pod trees are also called long-tailed cassia because of the 90 cm (3 ft) seed pods that hang down from their branches.

African mahogany
(Khaya grandifoliola)
Timber from this tree is prized for its reddish-brown hue and durability. It is used to make fine, strong furniture.

Emin's strophanthus
(Strophanthus eminii)
The soft leaves of strophanthus are often used as toilet paper!

Parrot plant *(Impatiens niamniamensis)*
Also known as the Congo cockatoo, the flowers of this plant dangle like tropical birds. They have developed bright hues to attract insects for pollination.

Wild ginger
(Aframomum ngamikkense)

This species of wild ginger has just been discovered in a remote mountain range of the Congo.

Lantern plant
(Ceropegia albisepta)

Traditionally, this plant was used to quench thirst.

Lombi tree
(Dalbergia glandulosa)

Buttress roots around the trunk help this tree gather nutrients from the shallow rain forest soil and stabilize it.

Cinchona tree
(Cinchona officinalis)

This tree is one of the world's most important tree species because its bark provides a medicine to treat malaria. The Congo has the biggest cinchona forest on the planet.

Miracle fruit
(Synsepalum dulcificum)

This fruit is magical! For half an hour after eating it, everything—even the sourest lemon—tastes very sweet.

Wing-leaved wooden pear
(Schrebera trichoclada)

This sweet-scented tree is also known as wild jasmine.

African pear *(Dacryodes edulis)*

The African pear's skin is purple. The flesh inside is deep green, sweet, and delicious.

Caramulla schweinfurthii
(Orbea schweinfurthii)
These flowers are very stinky! They smell like rotting fruit. This is a clever trick to attract flies looking for fruit on which to lay eggs. When the disappointed flies move to another flower, pollination is completed.

African blackwood
(Dalbergia melanoxylon)
The timber from this dark tree can be used to make musical instruments.

Polished star
(Duvalia polita)
These plants are only 10 cm (4 in) high and have spines on their stems to protect them against grazing animals.

Huernia *(Huernia verekeri)*
Huernia is a drought-resistant succulent. This means that parts of the plants store water—a feature that allows them to survive in very dry conditions.

Dorstenia benguellensis
(Dorstenia verdickii De Wild)
Many plants can only live in one habitat. Others, like this dorstenia, are much more adaptable and can thrive in grassland, forest, among rocks, and even in swamps.

Monadenium echinulata
(Euphorbia echinulata)
During the dry season, this plant looks like a chunk of wood buried in the sand. When the rains arrive, a stem and flowers sprout from this woody root.

Blood lily *(Scadoxus multiflorus)*
Powdered blood lilies were once used to catch fish! Sprinkled into the water, a chemical reaction takes place that paralyzes the fish so hunters can lift them straight out of the water.

ZAMBIA

Zambia is a landlocked country that has a rich mixture of habitats, the largest being grassland that is dotted with trees. But there are also wetlands, seasonally flooded swamps, farmland, hills, and valleys. Zambia does not receive sufficient rain to create dense rain forests. Instead, it has open, dry forests that grow on sandy soil.

The tropics have only two seasons each year—the wet season and the dry season. In Zambia, the rains occur from November to March, while the other seven months experience very little rainfall. Plants need to grow quickly when the rain comes; they must produce flowers, be pollinated, and set seed before the hot sun returns and foliage is burned off in the heat.

The greatest diversity of plants is usually found on the banks of rivers and lakes, since these bodies of water can feed the plants all year around.

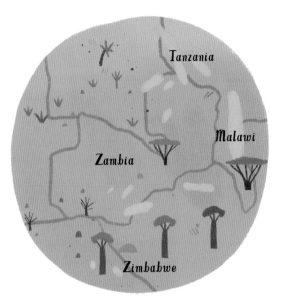

Red hot poker (*Kniphofia uvaria*)
Red hot pokers have become one of the world's best-loved garden flowers. Their common name comes from their similarity in appearance to a red-hot metal fire poker.

Candelabra tree (*Euphorbia ingens*)
The flowers of this plant produce lots of nectar and are an important feeding site for butterflies.

Dragon's head lily
(*Gladiolus dalenii*)
A dragon's head lily can grow to 2 m (6 ft 6 in) tall. The name *gladius* in the Latin word for "sword" and describes the sword-shaped leaves of the lily.

Zambia sausage tree
(*Kigelia africana*)
The salami-shaped fruits look good enough to eat but make sure you resist the temptation. These are safe to eat only once they've been dried and cooked.

African milk tree
(*Euphorbia trigona*)
When this plant's stem is damaged, a thick, white sap oozes out, giving it the name milk tree. But don't drink this milk as the sap is toxic!

23

CAPE FLORA

Fynbos describes the unique mountain, valley, as well as the scrubby coastal plains habitat and plants found at the southern tip of Africa. The fynbos is a biodiversity hotspot and home to 9,000 species. It includes vibrant proteas, vivid heathers, daisies, and restios—or reeds.

The plants of the fynbos are known as "fire-loving vegetation," which means that most benefit from occasional burning in order to remain healthy. Sometimes, this happens thanks to naturally occurring bushfires, while at other times, rangers deliberately light fires to keep the habitat in peak condition. This controlled burning is carefully planned so only small areas are burned. Scientists think that the fynbos needs to be scorched approximately every 15 years.

Knopbos
(Brunia noduliflora)

The seed heads of knopbos look like golf balls. They ripen on the plant for several years before the seeds finally emerge.

Flame lily *(Gloriosa superba)*

At a distance, these fiery lilies make the landscape look as if it is aflame.

Featherhead
(Phylica pubescens)

This plant smells slightly of cinnamon. Its glowing, feathery leaves are covered in hairs and attract insects.

Candy cane sorrel
(Oxalis versicolor)

The beautiful candy-like red stripes on the underside of the flower are visible only when the bloom is closed. Blooms are white on the upper side when fully open.

Cat's claw *(Cytinus sanguineus)*

Cat's claws are burglars! They send shoots out into the roots of other plants and take the water and nutrients from them.

Star window plant
(Haworthia cooperi)

Most of a star window plant is underground. The only visible parts are its strange see-through leaves.

Redlegs *(Berzelia abrotanoides)*

The fluffy ball-shaped heads can be dried and used in floristry.

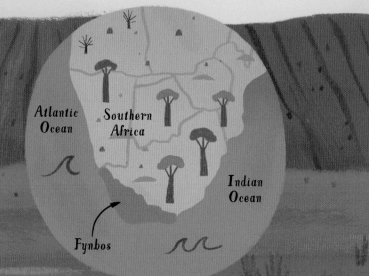

Atlantic Ocean

Southern Africa

Indian Ocean

Fynbos

Some fynbos plants drop seeds that remain in the ground until heat from fire sparks germination. Fire also releases minerals from mature plants that can be recycled by the sprouting seeds and allows sunlight to fall on to the young, growing shoots.

Fan aloe
(Kumara plicatilis)
Fan aloes have tough, moist leaves and a thick, spongy bark that help it survive most fynbos fires.

Candelabra lily
(Brunsvigia bosmaniae)
A mass flowering event brings an explosion of pink firework-like lilies from the dry earth.

Snow flower *(Syncarpha vestita)*
In springtime, these flowers look like snow has fallen on the mountains. Their leaves feel soft, like felt.

King protea *(Protea cynaroides)*
The glorious king protea is the national flower of South Africa. It provides food for the delicate Cape sugarbird *(Promerops cafer)*.

Coco de mer (*Lodoicea maldivica*)

These rare trees grow only on the Seychelle Islands. They produce the heaviest seed of any plant—each one weighs up to 30 kg (66 lb)!

Earring flower (*Trochetia boutoniana*)

Earring trees live only on the rocky slopes of a small peninsula in Mauritius.

Eelgrass (*Zostera capensis*)

Eelgrass grows in shallow seawater and forms large underwater meadows. It is an important food for marine animals such as turtles and dugongs.

Travelers' palm
(*Ravenala madagascariensis*)

Rain collects in the sheath surrounding the stem of a traveler's palm. In the dry season, water can be found here long after the last rains.

Silver madagascar palm
(*Bismarckia nobilis*)

These once grew only on Madagascar and are prized for their silver-blue foliage.

Porcupine tomato
(*Solanum, pyracanthos*)

Although this plant is related to tomatoes and potatoes, its fruit is poisonous. The stems are covered with bright orange spines, giving rise to its other name of "devil's thorn."

Flamboyant tree (*Delonix regia*)

The flamboyant tree is one of the most spectacular of all tropical trees. Its flowers can be yellow or bright red and are eaten by monkeys and lemurs.

INDIAN OCEAN

The Indian Ocean is home to many islands such as Mauritius, Zanzibar, and Sri Lanka. Most of the islands are a long distance from other land, and plants cannot easily extend their range when surrounded by sea. Some seeds, like the Coco de mer, can float to new locations, but finding a suitable new habitat it a matter of luck.

The Indian Ocean is bounded by Asia, Africa, Australia, and Antarctica so habitats range from tropical to the barren and frozen. Islands in the warm waters around the Equator are home to a far greater range of plants than those closer to the Antarctic, where winters are long and cold, making it difficult for plants to thrive.

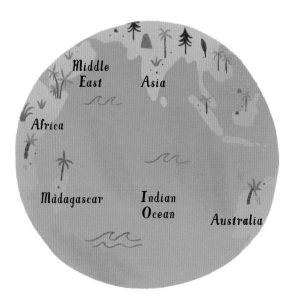

Sea hibiscus (*Hibiscus tiliaceus*)
Yellow, orange, or red? The shade of the blooms on this plant depends on the time of day. Flowers are yellow in the morning, orange by midday, and deep red by sunset!

Dragon tree (*Dracaena draco*)
When a branch is cut off this tree, red sap oozes from the wound. This is known as "dragon's blood."

Bois dentelle (*Elaeocarpus bojeri*)
Bois dentelle means "wood lace" in French and describes the plant's delicate white flowers. Fewer than 100 of these plants survive in the wild.

Octopus tree
(*Didierea madagascariensis*)
Octopus trees grow in southern Madagascar and are covered with long, sharp thorns. They grow in an area called the "Spiny Desert."

Wright's gardenia (*Rothmannia annae*)
This tree once lived throughout the Seychelles, but now it is only found on the island of Aride. Many people believe that it has the most beautifully scented flowers in the world.

NORTH AMERICA

North America is a continent of mountains, giant redwoods, spruce, pine, and fir woodlands, of tropical hardwood forests, deserts, and Great Plains. It is sometimes hard to imagine that the frozen landscape of Qikiqtaaluk in the far north of Canada is on the same continent as the tropical rain forests of Costa Rica. Between these two very different habitats are forests, deserts, and grassland, covering all three of the Earth's climate zones—tropical, temperate, and polar.

1 CANADA: BOREAL FOREST

Within the vast boreal forest trees grow whose bark makes perfect canoes, and others that seem to tremble. Precious wild rice and delicious cloudberries can be found here.

2 NORTH AMERICA: SUGAR MAPLE FOREST

The sap of these glorious trees gives us maple syrup. Tapping the trees is a way to source sugary food during the cold winter.

The vast boreal forests are one of the glories of North America. They contain the world's tallest trees and some extraordinary species of fungi. At first glance, the Sonoran Desert seems empty of all life but look closer and there is a wealth of plants and animals.

Many environments that were once threatened are now inside protected national parks, where visitors can come into close contact with nature, to walk, cycle, and take photographs. But other habitats are hidden from view. The giant kelp forests are one of North America's most interesting and important wildlife zones, yet few people see them because they lie in the cold waters of the Pacific. On the other side of the continent, plants surrounding the warm water of the Caribbean Islands thrive in their own unique environment, shaped by the sea and wind.

3 NORTH AMERICA and MEXICO: CHIHUAHUAN DESERT

Whole areas of the Chihuahuan Desert bloom gold with poppies and there are spectacular plants here that flower once in their lifetime and fade away afterward.

Northern wild rice
(Zizania palustris)

Horsetail
(Equisetum laevigatum)

Paper birch
(Betula papyrifera)

Eastern pasque flower
(Pulsatilla patens)

Strawberries and cream fungus
(Hydnellum peckii)

Red sea urchin
(Mesocentrotus franciscanus)

Common seal
(Phoca vitulina)

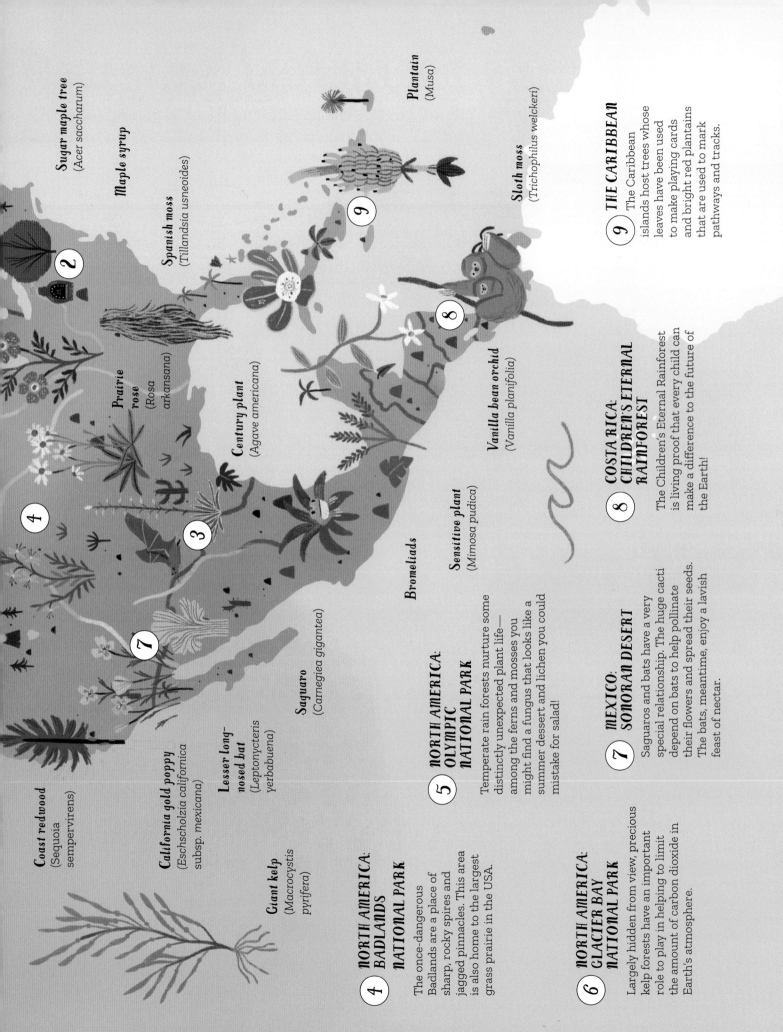

Sugar maple tree
(*Acer saccharum*)

Maple syrup

Spanish moss
(*Tillandsia usneoides*)

Plantain
(*Musa*)

Sloth moss
(*Trichophilus welckeri*)

Prairie rose
(*Rosa arkansana*)

Century plant
(*Agave americana*)

Vanilla bean orchid
(*Vanilla planifolia*)

California gold poppy
(*Eschscholzia californica* subsp. *mexicana*)

Lesser long-nosed bat
(*Leptonycteris yerbabuena*)

Coast redwood
(*Sequoia sempervirens*)

Bromeliads

Sensitive plant
(*Mimosa pudica*)

Saguaro
(*Carnegiea gigantea*)

Giant kelp
(*Macrocystis pyrifera*)

9 THE CARIBBEAN

The Caribbean islands host trees whose leaves have been used to make playing cards and bright red plantains that are used to mark pathways and tracks.

8 COSTA RICA: CHILDREN'S ETERNAL RAINFOREST

The Children's Eternal Rainforest is living proof that every child can make a difference to the future of the Earth!

5 NORTH AMERICA: OLYMPIC NATIONAL PARK

Temperate rain forests nurture some distinctly unexpected plant life—among the ferns and mosses you might find a fungus that looks like a summer dessert and lichen you could mistake for salad!

7 MEXICO: SONORAN DESERT

Saguaros and bats have a very special relationship. The huge cacti depend on bats to help pollinate their flowers and spread their seeds. The bats, meantime, enjoy a lavish feast of nectar.

4 NORTH AMERICA: BADLANDS NATIONAL PARK

The once-dangerous Badlands are a place of sharp, rocky spires and jagged pinnacles. This area is also home to the largest grass prairie in the USA.

6 NORTH AMERICA: GLACIER BAY NATIONAL PARK

Largely hidden from view, precious kelp forests have an important role to play in helping to limit the amount of carbon dioxide in Earth's atmosphere.

Paper birch (*Betula papyrifera*)
The strong, thin bark of this tree was used to make lightweight canoes that could be carried overland.

BOREAL FOREST, CANADA

Boreal forest is the largest land-based biome in the world. A biome is a community of plants and animals living in a similar natural habitat. The boreal is in North America and also Asia, Europe, and most of Scandinavia. The forest wraps around the Earth, just south of the Arctic Circle, and has long, freezing winters. Many plants become dormant in low temperatures. Their growing season is spring and summer but as these are short, plants grow very slowly.

Velvet leaf blueberry
(*Vaccinium myrtilloides*)
This is one of the most useful plants in the forest. Deer nibble the leaves, butterflies feed on the nectar, and many animals eat the ripe berries.

Trembling aspen
(*Populus tremuloides*)
Aspen leaves attach to trees on long, flexible stalks. In the wind, the leaves move and twist, meaning that the whole tree seems to quiver, giving it the name "trembling aspen."

Cloudberry
(*Rubus chamaemorus*)
Ripe fruits are a preferred food of grizzly bears.

Touch-me-not balsam
(*Impatiens capensis*)
The balsam seeds grow in a tightly packed pod. When the seeds are ripe, the pod pops violently—like a burst balloon—and propels the seeds into the air.

Eastern pasque flower
(*Pulsatilla patens*)
Early voyagers to Northern Canada used their dried leaves to make tea.

Rubber rabbitbrush
(*Ericameria nauseosa*)
Rabbitbrush flowers make bright yellow dyes for cloth. Scientists are now experimenting with the plant's sticky sap to produce a type of rubber for use by people with latex allergies.

Beaver (*Castor canadensis*)
Beavers are the architects of the woods. They use branches to build dams on rivers and help control flooding.

The Wood Buffalo National Park is the most ecologically complete example of the Great Plains boreal grassland ecosystem of North America. It was created just over 100 years ago to provide a home for wood bison, a species that was almost extinct. Since then, the bison, also called buffalo, population has grown together with the trees and plants under the protection of the park.

Great Slave Lake

Wood Buffalo National Park.

Lake Athabasca

Tamarack tree
(Larix laricina)
Tamaracks can tolerate super-cold conditions down to -65 °C (-85 °F).

Reindeer lichen (Cladonia rangiferina)
Also called reindeer moss, this is the main food for caribou. They use their hooves to dig through snow to reach the fresh lichen beneath. Lichen is not a plant but a colony of algae and fungi living together.

Wood bison
(Bison bison athabascae)
Bison were once hunted for meat and skins. They were almost extinct in the nineteenth century and were saved by conservationists, who moved them to specially protected areas.

Northern wild rice
(Zizania palustris)
Wild rice has an important place in the diet and culture of many Indigenous people. It grows in shallow water with only the seed heads showing above the surface and is harvested by canoe.

Morel (Morchella esculenta)
Never pick mushrooms without an expert guide! Cooked, these are a delicious edible mushroom but they are poisonous when raw.

Taconic
Mountains

New York

Oyster mushroom
(*Pleurotus ostreatus*)
Edible, tasty oyster
mushrooms grow on
decaying maples.

Purple Joe-Pye weed
(*Eutrochium purpureum*)
This is an important food
plant to the caterpillars of
many moths. After hatching,
the adult moths feed on its
rich nectar.

Heartleaf foamflower
(*Tiarella cordifolia*)
These grow well in the shade
created by maple trees. The
feathery white flowers look
like foam on water.

White turtlehead
(*Chelone glabra*)
The flower is shaped like
the head of a tortoise.

eysuckle
pervirens)
ds feed on the
s rich nectar
short summer
Vermont.

Black-eyed Susan
(*Rudbeckia hirta*)
These sunny flowers
appear in late summer.

Dutchman's breeches (*Dicentra cucullaria*)
This is named after the flowers' similarity
to the short white trousers worn by early
Dutch settlers in North America.

Sweet syrup
A healthy tree can produce 60 l (16 gallons) of syrup every year.

Food for all
Maples are browsed by moose, white-tailed deer, and snowshoe hare.

SUGAR MAPLE FOREST, TACONIC MOUNTAINS, VERMONT

Sugar maple trees (*Acer saccharum*) are native to northeast North America. They can form whole forests and live for more than 150 years. Maples are deciduous and have green and then spectacular red, orange, and yellow leaves. Their seeds will not germinate until they have spent a winter at temperatures around 0°C (32°F).

Trees use a thick, sticky sap to carry food and water from the roots up to the leaves. Along with lots of other nutrients, sap contains natural sugar. Maple sap contains more sugar than most tree species. When a hole is made into the tree, sap oozes slowly out. This is called "tapping" the tree and was a way for Indigenous people to produce sugar. The sap is boiled to remove the water and what is left is golden maple syrup—perfect for pouring over pancakes! The sugar maple is Canada's national tree and is also found on the Canadian flag.

CHIHUAHUAN DESERT, NORTH AMERICA

This is the largest desert in North America. It stretches from Central Mexico in the south, across the border, and into three US states. Around 3,000 plants species have been discovered here so far, making it probably the world's most biodiverse desert. About one third of the world's cactus species live in this place.

It's easy to think that all deserts are hot, but the Chihuahuan Desert is actually a "cold desert." The temperature at night can fall to 0°C (32°F) and the average highest summer temperature is around 29°C (84°F). A desert is any area that receives less than 25 cm (10 in) of rainfall in a year. The Chihuahuan Desert sits between two mountain ranges that create an effect called the "rain shadow." This happens when high mountains protect nearby low-lying land from the worst weather conditions. They shelter the rain-shadow area from storms, strong winds, and heavy rainfall.

Mexican gold poppy
(*Eschscholzia californica* subsp. *mexicana*)
These poppies bloom together after heavy rain. They carpet the desert in gold.

Century plant
(*Agave americana*)
A century plant lives for 25 years. Just before it dies, the plant produces a 9 m (30 ft)-high stalk that's covered in flowers.

Teddy bear cholla
(*Cylindropuntia bigelovii*)
The teddy bear cholla looks very cute but this plant is definitely not for cuddling. The "hairs" are actually long, thin, super-sharp spines!

Chuparosa
(Justicia californica)
These plants sometimes freeze to the ground on cold desert nights but soon recover when the temperature rises.

Creosote bush
(Larrea tridentata)
These bushes are described as the backbone of the desert. They provide food, firewood, and medicine. It is the food plant of 22 species of bee.

Distant scorpionweed
(Phacelia distans)
Traditionally, the leaves of this plant are cooked and eaten by Indigenous people.

Spanish bayonet
(Yucca torreyi)
The leathery leaves of this plant were once used to make cloth, sandals, and mats.

Brittlebush *(Encelia farinosa)*
Brittlebrush stems snap when bent.

Ghost flowers
(Mohavea confertiflora)
Ghost flowers do not produce any nectar—but they mimic a plant that does! They evolved to look like sand-blazing star (*Mentzelia involucrate*). Bees visit ghost flowers looking for food, but instead they simply transfer pollen.

Globemallow (*Sphaeralcea coccinea*)
Globemallow leaves were once used to line the bottom of shoes to ease pain caused by foot blisters.

Foxtail barley (*Hordeum jubatum*)
Each plant can produce up to 200 seeds, which allows the plant to spread very quickly.

Horsetail
(*Equisetum laevigatum*)
Horsetails shared the world with dinosaurs! They are an ancient plant form that first appeared around 200 million years ago.

White baneberry
(*Actaea pachypoda*)
Like a many-eyed alien from a sci-fi movie, baneberries stare in unexpected directions! Their other name is "doll's-eyes"—and it is not difficult to see why.

Scarlet beeblossom
(*Oenothera suffrutescens*)
The plant grows in large colonies and has fragrant flowers. It had been used in folk medicine to stop vomiting.

Scarlet swamp milkweed
(*Asclepias incarnate*)
Milkweed is the key food plant for the caterpillars of the monarch butterfly (*Danaus plexippus*).

Tufted evening primrose (*Oenothera caespitosa*)
These flowers open at sunset, ready to be pollinated by night-flying moths. They close again when the sun rises.

BADLANDS NATIONAL PARK, NORTH AMERICA

South Dakota is the traditional home of the Lakota people. They called it *mako sica*—"bad land." The jagged canyons, sticky mud during the rains, drought, and extreme temperatures meant that life was not easy for the people, plants, or wildlife that lived there. Today, the landscape is still being eroded by wind and water. Every year, the hills lose around 2.4 cm (1 in) in height.

The 990 sq km (245,000 acres) of the Badlands National Park are home to bison, bighorn sheep, and prairie dogs. The high hills contain few plants, but the lower altitudes are well known for mixed-grass prairies, open grasslands with few trees, and plenty of wild flowers. Approximately half of the park is covered with ankle- and waist-high grasses. It is one of the most threatened habitats in America because humans have accidentally introduced new plant species that compete with the natural grasses.

Poison ivy *(Toxicodendron radicans)*
Ouch! When poison ivy is crushed it releases oil that causes rashes, bumps, and blisters on human skin.

Prairie rose
(Rosa arkansana)
The fruit of this plant is an excellent source of vitamin C. It can be eaten raw or made into syrups or preserves.

Fireweed
(Chamaenerion angustifolium)
Fireweed is often the first plant to reappear after a bushfire.

Western wheatgrass
(Pascopyrum smithii)
Western wheatgrass is the dominant grass of the prairie. It is food for grazing animals such as bison.

TEMPERATE RAIN FOREST

The Olympic National Park has several distinctly different ecosystems, including glacier-capped mountains, wild coastline, and rain forests.

Woodlands on the west side of the park are some of the wettest places in North America—with a rainfall of 3.3–4.2 m (11–14 ft) each year. These are "temperate" rain forests, which means they have as much rain as the Amazon but exist in a climate where temperatures are more moderate. The forest has a jungle-like feel. Mosses, ferns, and lichen grow over the branches of large, old coniferous and deciduous trees. Some of the tallest trees in the world can be found here.

The ground is carpeted with ferns. Fallen trees become home to communities of fungi, small mammals, amphibians, and insects. Decomposing leaves and animal droppings make perfect food plants for the yellow Pacific banana slug (*Ariolimax columbianus*), which measures 25 cm (10 in) long! The slugs spread spores and seeds as they eat and help nourish the soil with their droppings.

Lettuce lichen
(*Lobaria oregana*)
Pieces of this lettuce leaf-like lichen are often seen on the forest floor, but they grow high up in the canopy and are dislodged by strong winds.

Pacific bleeding heart
(*Dicentra formosa*)
This plant produces long lines of heart-shaped flowers that hang elegantly from thin stems.

Salmonberry (*Rubus spectabilis*)
These berries ripen at the same time as the salmon leave the sea and move into rivers to breed. Salmon were often eaten with the berries—a custom that gave the plant its name.

Calypso orchid
(*Calypso bulbosa*)
Calypso orchids can be found in temperate rain forests around the world. They can't survive in bright sunshine and like to grow in the shade of giant conifers.

Vancouver groundcone
(*Kopsiopsis hookeri*)
The groundcone is a parasite that attaches itself to other plants underground. They grow in a range of different shades, such as yellow, brown, and purple.

Western hemlock
(Tsuga heterophylla)
The "Forest of Giants" contains some of the tallest trees in the North America, including the western hemlock. Their crushed needles smell like grapefruit.

Broadleaf lupine
(Lupinus latifolius)
Broadleaf lupines have roots that spread widely. They are often planted after a landslide as they bind the soil and help stop erosion.

Strait of Juan de Fuca

Olympic
National Park

Washington State

Pacific pink rhododendron
(Rhododendron macrophyllum)
The pink rhododendron is the official flower of Washington State.

Strawberries and cream fungus
(Hydnellum peckii)
Also called "devil's tooth," this fungus is at home in both a fairy tale and a horror movie. The "bleeding" is not actually strawberry sauce but sap.

Western columbine *(Aquilegia formosa)*
Seeds of the western columbine were once crushed and used as perfume.

KELP FOREST, GLACIER BAY NATIONAL PARK

Mysterious kelp forests are found in the ocean. Kelp is a seaweed and part of the brown algae family. Algae appeared on Earth long before the plants we see on land evolved.

Alaska

Glacier Bay National Park

Sea otters (Enhydra lutris)
Otters help keep the forest healthy by feeding on the sea urchins that eat the kelp.

Dabberlocks (Alaria esculenta)
A seaweed with a distinctive taste that is eaten fresh or cooked.

Sugar kelp (Saccharina latissima)
Sugar kelp contains a chemical called mannitol, a natural sugar. Traditionally, dried sugar kelp was used to sweeten food.

Common seal (Phoca vitulina)
These seals hunt fish, crustaceans, and mollusks in the kelp forest.

Giant kelp (Macrocystis pyrifera)
There are more than 10,000 seaweed species and 300 different types of kelp. This is the largest and can live for up to seven years.

Hidey holes
Rich kelp forests provide excellent hiding places for small fish.

Kelp is the largest of these underwater life forms. It lives in colonies of greenish-brown leaves called "blades" and can stretch up to 60 m (200 ft) from seabed to the surface of the ocean. The blades divide into fronds as they reach the surface and are kept afloat by "bladders" or pockets of air and gas. There, they feed by photosynthesis. These colonies are called forests. They are found in cold, shallow, coastal waters. Some animals live at the forest's "canopy" level, some hunt among the kelp blades, while others forage on the seafloor. Astonishingly, kelp forests produce 20 percent of the world's oxygen.

Harlequin duck
(Histrionicus histrionicus)
Harlequin ducks eat small crabs and insects.

Tasty and nutritious
Kelp is nutrient-rich, contains lots of minerals, and is delicious! It has been eaten for centuries in Japan, China, Korea, New Zealand, and Scandinavia.

Bull kelp
(Nereocystis luetkeana)
Bull kelp grows at a rate of 18 cm (7 in) a day. It lives for one year.

Red sea urchins
(Mesocentrotus franciscanus)
Sea urchins are slow-moving animals that devour algae. Kelp forests make a perfect feast, but they can be destroyed by high numbers of urchins.

Oarweed
(Laminaria digitata)
The blade in this species of brown alga is the shape of a boat's oar.

Holding on
A holdfast is a root-like tangle that fixes kelp to the seafloor or to rocks. Its powerful grip can stay firm against most storms.

SONORAN DESERT, MEXICO

The Sonoran Desert is the hottest desert in Mexico, and it is known for the saguaro cactus. Cacti are desert specialists. The secret of their success is that they store rainwater in their stems, which expand visibly, for use in periods of drought. They also conserve the water they have.

While the leaves of most plants are covered in tiny holes called "stoma" that constantly release moisture into the air, the leaves of cacti have evolved to become spines. Spines do not lose water or absorb heat. They do protect the cactus from animals.

The saguaro cactus has large branches that are known as "side arms." Some huge saguaros have as many as 150 arms, all of which will bear fruit. They grow very slowly, getting larger only when water is available. In dry years, they don't grow at all. The saguaro can be 12 m (40 ft) tall and live for 150 years.

Elf owl
(Micrathene whitneyi)
Elf owls are the size of house sparrows. They nest in old holes made by gila woodpeckers *(Melanerpes uropygialis)*.

White winged doves
(Zenaida asiatica)
Saguaro specialists, these birds rely on the cacti for food and water during their breeding season. In return, they pollinate and spread the seeds of the saguaro.

Home to many
Throughout its long life cycle, the saguaro provides food and shelter to a host of species.

Gila woodpecker *(Melanerpes uropygialis)*
Gila woodpeckers build their nests by drilling holes into a saguaro cactus and making a cavity in which they lay their eggs.

USA

Sonoran
Desert

Mexico

Strong spines
The spines of the
saguaro are almost
as strong as steel and
can grow up to 7 cm
(3 in) long. Many desert
animals have been found
with cactus spines stuck
in their skin.

Lesser long-nosed bats
(*Leptonycteris yerbabuenae*)
These bats spend their
days sleeping in caves and
come out at night to feed on
saguaro nectar and pollinate
the cacti.

Packed with seeds
Most desert animals feed on
saguaro fruit. Each fruit contains
around 2,000 seeds, which are
dispersed in animal droppings.

Crested saguaro
This is a rare form of
saguaro with a unique
fan shape.

Fleeting flowers
Each cactus can
produce 100 white,
waxy flowers a year,
but each bloom lasts
for only one day and
opens only at night.

43

Darth Vader plant
(*Aristolochia salvadorensis*)
This is a rare rain forest plant with a flower that looks just like the well-known *Star Wars* character.

Vanilla orchid (*Vanilla planifolia*)
Vanilla orchids grow in Central American rain forests and produce fruit in long, thin fruit pods. Dried pods produce natural vanilla, a delicious spice popular in ice cream and chocolate.

Flying goldfish plant
(*Columnea microcalyx*)
These "fishy" flowers grow in the highest parts of the reserve, in an area called cloud forest.

Coral tree
(*Erythrina poeppigiana*)
Coral trees have very soft wood that rots easily. Old trees have many holes in their thick trunks. These are perfect nesting places for toucans and parrots.

Sensitive plant
(*Mimosa pudica*)
The leaves of these shy plants close up tightly as soon as they are touched.

CHILDREN'S ETERNAL RAIN FOREST, COSTA RICA

This is one of the most biodiverse habitats on Earth and a miracle of conservation. It is a reserve saved from destruction entirely by the actions of children. In 1987, a schoolteacher from Sweden visited Costa Rica and was horrified to see its forests being cut down. When she told her pupils about the deforestation, they decided to try to stop it. The children sold homemade cakes and cards, washed cars, and donated pocket money, and eventually saved sufficient funds to buy a small area of forest. Other schools joined in to raise more funds and buy more forest.

Since then, children from 44 countries have created one of the world's most important reserves. Their efforts have paid off. Now, 30 completely new tree species have been discovered inside the reserve. It is home to 450 species of bird and has the largest population of orchid species in one location on Earth.

Pacaya palm
(*Chamaedorea tepejilote*)
Some plants grow well inside the dark forest. The pacaya palm leaves die if they are exposed to too much sunlight.

Red-eyed tree frog
(*Agalychnis callidryas*)
Tree frogs spend their lives above the ground. They hunt small insects and lay their eggs in the small pools of water inside bromeliads.

Costa Rica

Bromeliad
Bromeliads are "epiphytes"—plants that grow on other plants. The leaves of bromeliads form a cup that catches the rain and provides water for the plant.

Madras thorn tree
(*Pithecellobium dulce*)
Cloud forests are cooler than lowland rain forests and their plants are usually not as tall. The Madras thorn tree grows to only about 10 m (33 ft).

Sloth moss (*Trichophilus welckeri*)
Sloths are camouflaged against the trees by the algae or "sloth moss" that grows on their fur. Some sloths look distinctly green!

THE CARIBBEAN

The tropical Caribbean Sea is the western part of the Atlantic Ocean. The climate is warm and wet, which is a perfect combination for plant life. There is a wonderful variety of habitats scattered around more than 2,000 islands. Vegetation is lush and varied— orchids, bromeliads, tree ferns, and figs are plentiful.

Although trees are also diverse, much of the Caribbean's original forest has been cut down to make way for people, agriculture, and tourism. This is a problem made worse by the hurricanes that strike the Caribbean every year. June to November is the hurricane season, when strong winds of up to 240 km/h (150 mph) batter the islands and can flatten much of the vegetation. Plants need to grow very quickly so they can produce seeds before another storm strikes. Many of the plants in the region are endemic, that is, unique to their islands.

Peacock flower *(Caesalpinia pulcherrima)*
This is the national flower of Barbados. It is an important nectar source for the Caribbean's hummingbirds.

Custard apple *(Annona squamosa)*
Despite the name, this fruit is not an apple but it certainly tastes like custard. Ripe fruit are kept very cold and served with ice cream for a much-loved Caribbean dessert.

Plantain *(Musa)*
Plantains are a type of banana that contain very little sugar. They are not eaten as fruit but cooked just like potatoes—fried, mashed, or roasted.

Spanish moss *(Tillandsia usneoides)*
Spanish moss lives high on tree branches, chimneys, and even telephone wires. It has no roots and survives by photosynthesis and absorbing water directly from the air.

Autograph tree
(Clusia rosea)

Leaves of autograph trees are so strong that it is possible to carve words into their waxy surface with a fingernail or sharp stick. They have also been used to make playing cards.

North America

Atlantic Ocean

Caribbean Islands

Caribbean Sea

Central America

South America

Caribbean heliconia
(Heliconia caribaea)

Before roads were built, wild plantain, the bright red heliconia, were planted alongside tracks so voyagers could find their way around the islands —ingenious!

Ackee *(Blighia sapida)*

Ackee trees were taken from Africa to the islands about 250 years ago. The trees produce fruit all year around and have become one of the Caribbean's most popular foods.

Cashew
(Anacardium occidentale)

Originally from South America, cashews have become so popular that the trees have been planted all around the Caribbean.

Star of Bethlehem
(Hippobroma longiflora)

The sap in a star of Bethlehem is so poisonous that people need to wear gloves before touching the plant.

Sea grape *(Coccoloba uvifera)*

Sea grape trees grow close to the beach of most Caribbean islands. They are one of the few trees that can grow in the salty, sandy earth.

SOUTH AMERICA

Around one third of all the known plants on Earth are found in South America! It has the greatest plant diversity of all the continents with more than 100,000 species recorded so far. The figure is so high because South America has such an impressive range of habitats to explore—the Amazon rain forest, Andes Mountains, grasslands, and deserts provide very different conditions for plants and animals.

People first arrived in South America around 12,000 years ago, which is a very short time in the history of our species. They discovered unfamiliar plants that supplied food, medicine, and building materials—like those used to construct the fantastic floating villages on Lake Titicaca. Some plant products that were once only known locally, such as delicious pineapple and Brazil nuts, went far beyond South America to be enjoyed all across the world.

1 VENEZUELA and the GUIANAS: GIANT AMAZON WATER LILY

Almost yummy enough to eat, flowers of the giant water lily smell of pineapple!

2 COLUMBIA: MANGROVE HABITAT

Extraordinary mangrove forests are a "blue carbon" habitat. This means they trap carbon and help fight climate change.

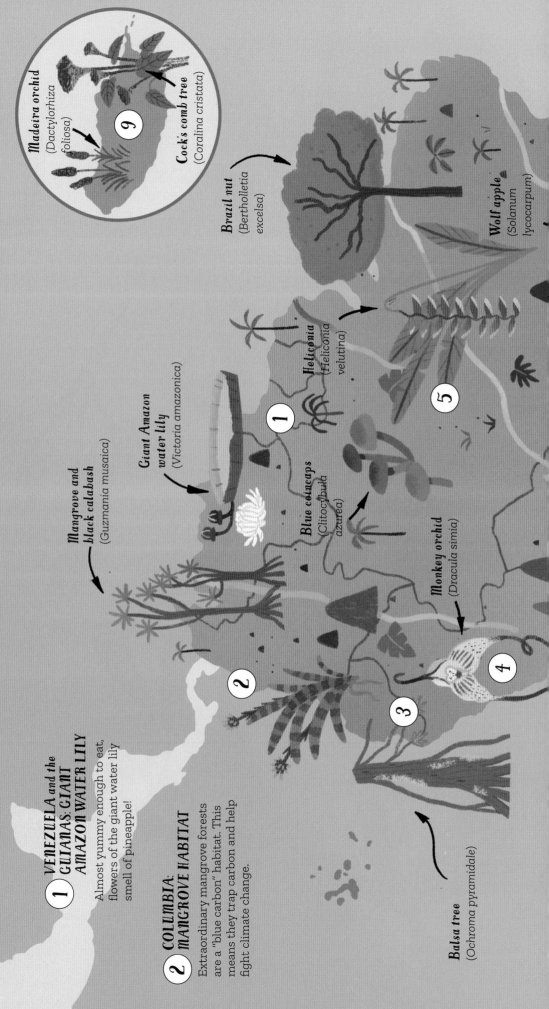

Madeira orchid
(*Dactylorhiza foliosa*)

Cock's comb tree
(*Coralina cristata*)

Brazil nut
(*Bertholletia excelsa*)

Wolf apple
(*Solanum lycocarpum*)

Heliconia
(*Heliconia velutina*)

Mangrove and black calabash
(*Guzmania musaica*)

Giant Amazon water lily
(*Victoria amazonica*)

Blue coincaps
(*Clitocybula azurea*)

Monkey orchid
(*Dracula simia*)

Balsa tree
(*Ochroma pyramidale*)

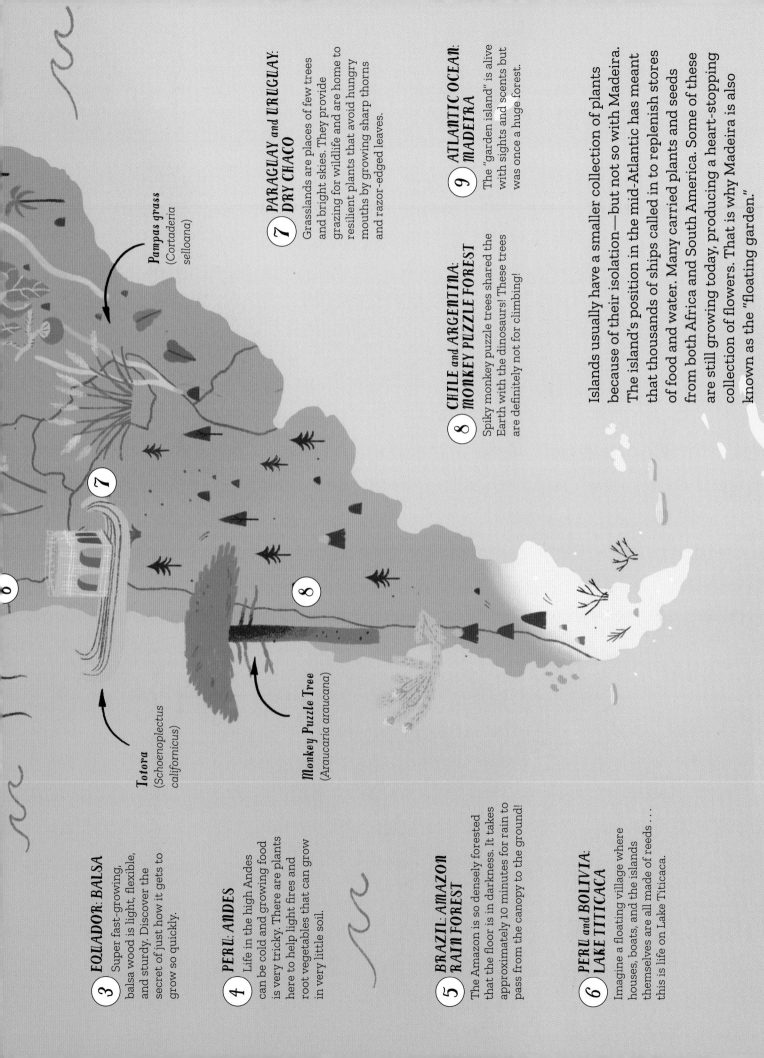

③ EQUADOR: BALSA

Super fast-growing, balsa wood is light, flexible, and sturdy. Discover the secret of just how it gets to grow so quickly.

④ PERU: ANDES

Life in the high Andes can be cold and growing food is very tricky. There are plants here to help light fires and root vegetables that can grow in very little soil.

⑤ BRAZIL: AMAZON RAIN FOREST

The Amazon is so densely forested that the floor is in darkness. It takes approximately 10 minutes for rain to pass from the canopy to the ground!

⑥ PERU and BOLIVIA: LAKE TITICACA

Imagine a floating village where houses, boats, and the islands themselves are all made of reeds ... this is life on Lake Titicaca.

Totora
(*Schoenoplectus californicus*)

Monkey Puzzle Tree
(*Araucaria araucana*)

Pampas grass
(*Cortaderia selloana*)

⑦ PARAGUAY and URUGUAY: DRY CHACO

Grasslands are places of few trees and bright skies. They provide grazing for wildlife and are home to resilient plants that avoid hungry mouths by growing sharp thorns and razor-edged leaves.

⑧ CHILE and ARGENTINA: MONKEY PUZZLE FOREST

Spiky monkey puzzle trees shared the Earth with the dinosaurs! These trees are definitely not for climbing!

⑨ ATLANTIC OCEAN: MADEIRA

The "garden island" is alive with sights and scents but was once a huge forest.

Islands usually have a smaller collection of plants because of their isolation—but not so with Madeira. The island's position in the mid-Atlantic has meant that thousands of ships called in to replenish stores of food and water. Many carried plants and seeds from both Africa and South America. Some of these are still growing today, producing a heart-stopping collection of flowers. That is why Madeira is also known as the "floating garden."

GIANT AMAZON WATER LILY, VENEZULA and the GUIANAS

The giant water lily (*Victoria amazonica*) is one of South America's natural wonders. The leaves—or pads—can measure 3 m (10 ft) across and support the weight of a small child. They grow to cover the entire surface of a river, from bank to bank. The pads are the visible part of the lily, and

Leafy guttering
Every leaf has a spout that allows rainwater to escape. Without this, the leaf would sink.

Spiky leaves
Each leaf has an edge covered in spines to deter fish from nibbling them.

Scarab beetle
(*Scarabaeidae*)
This beetle carries pollen from flower to flower.

Protector plants
Caiman are cannibalistic. Young caiman often climb on the lily leaves for safety when a larger adult is nearby.

Taking cover
Fish often hide in the shade of a floating lily leaf when a bird predator is spotted.

are anchored to stems and roots underwater. The roots grow on the riverbed up to 10 m (33 ft) below. Pads are very buoyant. The spiny underside of the leaves trap air that helps them float.

The lilies have evolved alongside a group of beetles called scarabs (*Scarabaeidae*). The rich nectar provides food for the scarabs and, in return, the scarabs pollinate the lilies. If either of them were to become extinct, the remaining one would likely also disappear. Lilies bloom at the same time, producing a strong scent that attracts the beetles from a long distance.

Striated heron
(*Butorides striata*)
Floating leaves are an ideal hunting platform for herons looking for fish.

Caught in a trap
The flowers close at dawn, trapping the pollinating beetles until the next evening.

Night bloomers
White flowers open at night and bloom for just three days. Once they have released pollen, they turn pink.

Underwater skeleton
The underside of the lily leaf is a complicated arrangement of stem branches. They work like a skeleton to keep the leaf strong.

MANGROVE HABITAT, COLOMBIA

The tropical mangrove forests of Colombia thrive in conditions that would kill most plants. There are at least 50 species of mangrove tree and they grow in saltwater, in the narrow band of mud between high and low tides of the ocean.

Acai palm
(Euterpe oleracea)
Acai palms grow on the edge of the mangroves and produce around 900 berries each year. They look and taste like blackberries.

Black calabash
(Guzmania musaica)
The black calabash avoids salt by living high up on the trunks of other trees.

Oncilla *(Leopardus tigrinus)*
The oncilla is a shy, nocturnal predator that lives in dense undergrowth.

Spiked mangrove seeds
Mangrove seeds are long and pointed, like spears. They drop from branches into the fertile mud below.

Bare-throated tiger heron
(Tigrisoma mexicanum)
This heron is a crab-hunting specialist.

Beach bean
(Canavalia rose)
Beach beans are climbing vines that use mangrove trees as support.

52

The Esmeraldas-Pacific mangroves cover some 6,500 sq km (2,500 sq mi) and provide a home to various unique wildlife species. At high tide, mangrove swamps sit in deep water. As the tide goes out, it exposes the stilt-like aerial roots that help support the trees and absorb oxygen from the air.

Surviving in this tidal habitat is all about salt-tolerance. Many plants die if their roots are trapped in seawater—but not so with mangroves. They filter out salt, stopping it from entering their roots, or else they "sweat" out the salt through their leaves. Mangrove forests also help prevent the sea tides eroding the land.

Panama
Venezuela
Esmeraldas-Pacific Colombia mangroves
Colombia
Ecuador
Brazil
Peru

Black mangrove (*Avicennia germinans*)
These grow just above the high tide in mangrove forests. They cannot tolerate salt so well as other mangrove plants.

American crocodile
(*Crocodylus acutus*)
American crocodiles live on the coast in saltwater and hunt in the mangroves.

Button mangrove
(*Conocarpus erectus*)
This mangrove produces clusters of fruit that look like the wooden buttons used to fasten clothing.

Mangrove tree crab (*Aratus pisonii*)
At low tide, tree crabs hunt on exposed mud. When the tide comes in, they climb up into the trees away from the water.

BALSA, ECUADOR

The Guayas River Forest in Western Ecuador is a tropical dry forest that contains a very special tree called the balsa. This is a native species that provides one of the lightest timbers in the world. Balsa is extremely strong and is used to make boats and surf boards and was once used to build the frames of full-size airplanes.

Kinkajou *(Potos flavus)*
Kinkajous are small, nocturnal mammals that live in the treetops. They use their incredible 13cm (5 in)-long tongue to feed on nectar and are the main pollinator of balsa flowers.

Choco toucan *(Ramphastos brevis)*
Balsa fruit is a preferred food of these toucans. They often nest inside the rotting trunks of old balsa trees.

Nectar-laden flowers
Balsa flowers produce enormous amounts of nectar. Each flower can contain a pool of nectar that is 2.5cm (1 in) deep.

Big leaves
Young balsa trees have very large leaves that accelerate photosynthesis and increase the speed of growth.

Balsa grows much faster than other trees because its wood contains huge cells that are full of water. Raw or "green" balsa wood cut from living trees is heavy because the cells are still very wet; 75 percent of its weight is water. Balsa needs to be completely dry before it becomes light and easy to cut.

Balsa can live for 40 years, but most trees are cut down at around eight years old. Only young trees produce soft wood. Older balsas become much harder and the original soft wood rots away.

Smoky-brown woodpecker
(Dryobates fumigatus)
The soft trunks of young balsa trees are home to wood-boring insects, so they are a perfect hunting ground for woodpeckers.

Guayas River Forest

Ecuador

Flying seed pods
Balsa trees produce pods that contain hundreds of seeds. Each seed has a long hair that catches the wind and blows it through the forest.

Toy airplane
Balsa's strength and lightness makes it a perfect building material for model airplanes. Ecuador produces most of the balsa used in model-making.

Wood structure
Under a microscope, balsa wood is full of air holes.

Dried wood
The word "balsa" means raft in Spanish. Dried balsa floats better than any other wood. Most balsa is now kiln-dried commercially.

ANDES, PERU

The Andes is the longest mountain range in the world. It runs the whole length of South America from the tropics almost down to the Antarctic. On a map, the high Peruvian mountains are close to the Amazonian lowland forest, where the temperature can reach 40°C (104°F). Up in the mountains, the 3,750 m (12,300 ft) altitude produces a habitat that feels more like the Arctic, especially at night. Plants that live here grow low to the ground and there are very few trees. Strong winds damage tall plants, so only short, hardy species can survive among the rocky slopes of the high country that locals call Tierra Helda, "the frozen land."

The lower sheltered valleys, by contrast, are protected from the worst of the mountain weather and support a much larger number of plants. In fact, the Andes even has a few small low-altitude forests.

Peru

Yareta (*Azorella compacta*)
The strange yareta lives at high altitude. It grows about 1.5 cm (0.6 in) a year in the cold conditions. Some are believed to be 3,000 years old,

Monkey orchid (*Dracula simia*)
Monkey orchids smell like oranges. Their spooky appearance is responsible for their local name of "dracula orchid."

Quinoa (*Chenopodium quinoa*)
Protein-rich quinoa is a native plant of the Andes. Its seeds have been eaten by humans and animals for thousands of years.

Vira vira *(Senecio canescens)*
The long hairs of vira vira plants are traditionally used to start fires.

"Old Man of the Andes"
(Oreocereus celsianus)
This cactus is covered in long, white hairs that look like a shaggy beard. The hairs protect the cactus from cold and the very bright sunlight found on high mountains.

Peruvian magic tree *(Cantua buxifolia)*
The Peruvian magic tree was the sacred flower of the Incas and is now the national flower of Peru.

Queen of the Andes
(Puya raimondii)
The Queen of the Andes is a rare plant that has its first flowers around the age of 80 years old. They appear on a long stem that can reach 15 m (50 ft) tall. After flowering, the plant dies.

Cassava
(Manihot esculenta)
Cassava can survive on dry, rocky ground with very little soil. The hard, plump roots are called manioc and can be made into flour or eaten as a vegetable.

Tall tree (Dinizia excelsa)
Some exceptional trees grow much taller than the canopy. They can reach a height of 70 m (230 ft) and form the emergent layer.

AMAZON RAIN FOREST, BRAZIL

Brazil is the most biodiverse country on Earth, and the Amazon rain forest is its star habitat. The forest is about half the size of Europe and contains around 20 percent of all known plant species.

Brazil nut
(Bertholletia excelsa)
Brazil nut trees were once used to produce a valuable red dye. It was so important commercially that the country was named after the tree.

Amazon moonflower
(Selenicereus wittii)
Moonflowers are one of only three cactus species that grow in the rain forest. Their white flowers open at night.

Venezuela
Colombia
Ecuador
Amazon rain forest
Peru
Bolivia
Brazil
Paraguay

Blue coincaps
(Clitocybula azurea)
Fungi are a vitally important part of the forest. They help decay fallen trees so their nutrients can pass back into the ecosystem.

Cacao (Theobroma cacao)
This is the Amazon's best-known tree. Cacao seeds are called cocoa beans and are used to make chocolate.

Red lips (Palicourea elata)
The flashy red "lips" are special leaves called "bracts" that attract insects to pollinate the tiny flowers inside.

Liana vine
Lianas are any woody vines that climb trees in order to reach the canopy.

Rain forest plants live at different levels within the forest. It helps to think of these as layers. The forest floor layer has fungi to break down plant matter. Most plants have their roots anchored in the soil but try to reach the light high above. They grow into the midlayer, called the under canopy, and produce a mass of leaves designed to catch whatever sunlight is available. The higher canopy layer of the forest is where sunlight falls. It is here that most fruit, flowers, and animals can be found. Topmost is the emergent layer, where highfliers like eagles perch. Rain forest trees are short-lived. When one dies, there is a race by nearby trees to reach the bright gap in the canopy above.

Parkia *(Parkia pendula)*
This tree is able to survive many weeks of waterlogged roots in the flooded forest.

Cannonball tree
(Couroupita guianensis)
These round fruits look like rusty cannonballs. They are a preferred food of peccaries *(Tayassuidae)*, which distribute the seeds in their droppings.

Heliconia *(Heliconia velutina)*
Heliconia leaves are used to wrap and cook or store food by rain-forest peoples.

Monkey brush
(Combretum rotundifolium)
These flowers produce high levels of nectar and are important feeding sites for hummingbirds and butterflies.

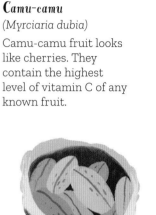

Camu-camu
(Myrciaria dubia)
Camu-camu fruit looks like cherries. They contain the highest level of vitamin C of any known fruit.

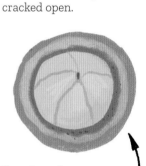

Tasty nuts
Brazils nuts ready to be cracked open.

Speedy pods
Brazil nuts grow in pods that can weigh 2 kg (5 lb). Falling pods can reach a speed of 80 km/h (50 mph) when they hit the ground.

Tasty cacao
A pod contains up to 50 beans. These are dried before being transformed into chocolate.

Titicaca is South America's largest freshwater lake. It is home to the Uros people, who live on handmade floating islands. Their homes and islands are made of reeds from the totora (*Schoenoplectus californicus* subsp. *tatora*) that grow in the lake.

Eat your greens!
The thickest part of totora stems can be eaten as a vegetable.

Reed dwellings
Most reed houses now have electricity supplied by solar panels.

Totora flowers
The reeds bloom in summer. However, most reproduce via vertical shoots that emerge from the underwater roots.

Many-colored rush tyrant
(*Tachuris rubrigastra*)
This gaudy bird lives among the reeds. They build their nests around strong stems and feed on insects that hide in the reed beds.

Guinea pig (*Cavia porcellus*)
The Uros people farm guinea pigs for food. They are not kept in pens but are free to run around the islands.

Totora can grow to 6 m (20 ft) in height. The reeds are cut and placed on top of a raft of reed roots that can be 2 m (6.5 ft) thick. A new layer of totora is added regularly. There are around 70 islands. Some have schools on them that are reached by boat.

Strong mountain winds create waves that erode the islands, and there is a risk of fire during the dry season. Each island lasts for around ten years. Fish is an important part of the diet. Islands are towed to other parts of the lake to find better fishing.

Lake Titicaca

Peru

Bolivia

Reed boat
Big reed boats can hold up to 20 people. They are used for fishing or covering long distances by water.

Caballitos de totora
These one-person boats were used for fishing. Their name means "little reed horses" because the rower straddled the boat as if on a horse. The boats are now used to ride waves.

Puna teal *(Spatula puna)*
These birds live at the edge of the lake so they can hide in the reeds if threatened.

Titicaca water frog
(Telmatobius culeus)
These frogs seem to have skin that is about three sizes too big for their bodies.

Titicaca grebe
(Rollandia microptera)
The Titicaca grebe lives in only a few high-altitude lakes and has lost the ability to fly.

DRY CHACO, PARAGUAY and ARGENTINA

The Dry Chaco, sometimes called the Gran Chaco, is lowland plain. Plains are largely flat landscapes. This plain is "alluvial," which means it was formed by sediment from rivers. The Gran Chaco means "Hunting Land" in the local Quechua language, a name that reflects the large number of animals grazing here.

This is an important habitat called savannah. Savannahs feature grasses and a few scattered trees. Grassland makes up around one third of the Earth's land surface, and it is under threat in South America from the grazing of cattle and planting of soy.

The Chaco Plain has some of the highest temperatures in South America, and the plants that thrive here have to be able to cope with the intense heat. Two permanent rivers flow through the plain and areas closer to them contain a wider range of plant life and rich forest.

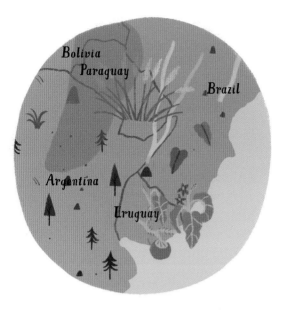

Pampas deer
(*Ozotoceros bezoarticus*)

The deer live among very tall grasses. They stand on their back legs to see above the grass.

Pink trumpet tree
(*Handroanthus impetiginosus*)

These are "honey trees." Their high levels of nectar attract bees, which then produce honey that is harvested by local people.

Blue passion flower
(*Passiflora caerulea*)

This is the national flower of Paraguay.

Marcela
(*Achyrocline satureioides*)

Dried flowers of marcela are burned during wedding celebrations to perfume the air.

Pineapple (*Ananas comosus*)

This delicious fruit was first found close to the Paraguay River.

Pampas grass (Cortaderia selloana)

This grows up to 3 m (10 ft) high. The edges of the leaves are razor sharp.

Yerba mate (Ilex paraguariensis)

This makes a traditional tea and is used in commercial soft drinks.

Wolf apple (Solanum lycocarpum)

The fruit of wolf apple trees is the most important food for maned wolves. The trees' seeds are dispersed in the wolves' droppings.

Cockspur coral tree (Erythrina crista-galli)

These trees always grow next to rivers.

Berberis (Berberis laurina)

Berberis plants are armed with rows of sharp spines to discourage hungry deer from eating them.

Ombú (Phytolacca dioica)

Ombús are the biggest trees in the pampas. They have soft, spongy timber that can be cut with a small knife.

Maned wolf (Chrysocyon brachyurus)

This animal eats wolf apples. It is mainly vegetarian.

Water hyacinth (Pontederia crassipes)

These plants float on the surface of the water, moving easily to new areas. They are highly invasive.

MONKEY PUZZLE FOREST, CHILE and ARGENTINA

Monkey puzzles are ancient trees, sometimes called "living fossils." They first appeared around 200 million years ago and are among the oldest of known tree species. Monkey puzzles are covered with hard, sharp leaves. Some experts think the leaves evolved this way to stop dinosaurs from eating them!

Conguillío National Park in Chile is home to a forest of monkey puzzles. Their official name is Chilean pine (*Araucaria araucana*) but few people use it. Their common name "monkey puzzle" comes from a comment made when the trees first arrived in Europe: an observer said that it would puzzle a monkey to climb the spiny branches.

In the monkey puzzle forests of Chile there are giant specimens that are 1,000 years old and 40 m (130 ft) tall. Outside of Chile, most trees are not yet fully grown.

Monkey puzzle tree
(*Araucaria araucana*)
In South America, monkey puzzle trees now grow only in a few forests.

Scottish refuge
Areas of Scotland have ideal soil and climate conditions for monkey puzzle trees. One secret glen has been planted with over 40 trees to help create a reserve population of this rare species.

Candelabra tree
(*Araucaria angustifolia*)
Candelabra trees are a close relative of monkey puzzles. They share the same habitat and are critically endangered.

Wild boar (*Sus scrofa*)
Wild boar have been introduced from Europe. They eat many of the fallen seeds before they have the chance to grow

The monkey puzzle forest is threatened by grazing livestock, overharvesting of their edible seeds, and wild fires. One recent fire destroyed more than a million trees.

Pacific
Ocean

Conguillio
National
Park

Chile

Argentina

Atlantic
Ocean

Edible seeds
The seeds were once part of the general diet for people in Chile.

Slender-billed parakeet
(*Enicognathus leptorhynchus*)
The parakeets use their long, thin bills to pick out seeds from the cones.

Long-lived leaves
Monkey puzzle branches are covered with sharp, triangular leaves that can live on the tree for 20 years.

Far-flung pollen
The flowers are pollinated by the wind. The pollen can be carried up to 10 km (6 mi).

Long-haired grass mouse
(*Abrothrix longipilis*)
The mice gather seeds and cache them around the forest to eat later. Sometimes they don't return and the seeds grow into new trees.

Seed cones
Monkey puzzle trees produce seeds inside huge, round cones. Each seed is about 4 cm (1.5 in) long.

Jacaranda (*Jacaranda mimosifolia*)

Jacaranda trees come from South America and have been planted in the middle of many of Madeira's towns and villages.

Canary foxglove
(*Digitalis sceptrum*)

Canary foxgloves grow in the forests in the middle of the island.

Lemon-scented jasmine
(*Jasminum azoricum*)

Every evening, the flowers produce a strong, sweet fragrance.

Madeira orchid
(*Dactylorhiza foliosa*)

Madeira has its own unique species of orchid. It is one of the many species on display at the island's orchid garden.

Malfurada
(*Hypericum grandifolium*)

This is an important source of nectar for Madeira's butterflies.

Pride of Madeira
(*Echium candicans*)

This is a biennial plant: it grows leaves in its first year but only forms flowers in its second year.

MADEIRA: THE GARDEN ISLAND

Madeira is part of Portugal but is located in the Atlantic Ocean close to the coast of Africa. No one lived on the islands until 600 years ago. Early explorers discovered a landscape covered in dense forests and named it Madeira, which means "wood" in Portuguese.

Madeira has two inhabited islands. They are located on the very top of a huge undersea volcano that goes 6 km (3.7 mi) down to the floor of the Atlantic Ocean. Volcanic soil contains high levels of minerals that are needed for growing plants.

Madeira has a warm climate and reasonable rainfall. Over millions of years, different kinds of seeds were carried there by the sea or by birds. These grew in the rich soil and evolved into plants not found elsewhere. Madeira holds an important flower festival every year and today is known as the "garden island."

Atlantic Ocean

Madeira

Cock's comb tree
(*Coralina cristata*)

The cock's comb tree produces so much nectar that is drips from the bright red flowers. This gave rise to its other name, the "cry baby" tree.

Verdelho grape

Grapes were introduced to Madeira in the fifteenth century. There are now many different varieties.

Lily-of-the-valley-tree (*Clethra arborea*)

These trees have long lines of bell-shaped flowers that hang down from thin stems.

ASIA

Asia is huge! It is the world's largest continent, covering almost one third of all land. It has the highest terrestrial mountains and is home to more than half the people on Earth. Little can live on the peaks of the Himalayas, but a remarkable number of plants have adapted to life in the nearby Gobi Desert. The Gobi's cold and dry climate is actually created by the surrounding mountains. Life for plants is always challenging in desert conditions. Much of the Arabian Desert is lifeless but its oases are rich habitats containing trees, fruits, and vegetation—they are important places for people and wildlife.

For plant biodiversity, nothing can rival rain forests. Those in Southeast Asia contain many species that are endemic. These forests once produced some of the world's most sought-after and expensive food items—spices. In fact, the Maluku Islands were known as the "spice islands."

Asia was also the original home of many of the most popular fruits—apples, bananas, pomegranates, and figs all evolved there. They have provided food for humans for thousands of years and are still important crops in the twenty-first century. In Japan, trees are so respected that one—the flowering cherry—even has its own festival every spring.

1 **JAPAN: CHERRY BLOSSOM**

In Japan, the cherry blossom is so important that it has its own festival in spring. Fossils suggest the first cherry trees appeared 44.3 million year ago.

2 **CHINA and MONGOLIA THE GOBI DESERT**

The Gobi is a cold, salty desert. Yet even in these extreme conditions there are plants that thrive. Some "steal" nutrients from the roots of other plants, others allow themselves to be blown by the wind to disperse their seeds.

Japanese cherry
(Cerasus jamasakura)

Salt bush
(Seidlitzia stocksii)

Morel
(Morchella esculenta)

Russian larch
(Larix sibirica)

Pomegranate
(Punica granatum)

Apple
(Malus spp.)

Apricot
(Prunus armeniaca)

Cinnamon
(*Cinnamomum cassia*)

Black moss

Wild leek
(*Allium tricoccum*)

Oil palm tree
(*Elaeis guineensis*)

⑨

⑧

Tamarisk
(*Tamarix arceuthoides*)

Vanilla bean orchid
(*Vanilla planifolia*)

Wood

④

⑦

Banana
(*Musa spp.*)

Date palm
(*Phoenix dactylifera*)

⑥

③ RUSSIA: VIRGIN KOMI FOREST

Komi is part of the ancient boreal forest. Beneath the trees are fungi that look like fingers and plants that are burned to keep away witches!

④ KAZAKHSTAN: APPLES

Sweet, tangy apples are eaten all over the world. They can be red, green, yellow, or pink and vary in size from grapefruit to golf ball. But where did they come from and how did we achieve so many varieties?

⑤ TURKEY and the CAUCASUS: POMEGRANATES

One of the first fruits to be cultivated by people, the jewel-like pomegranate has an important place in many cultures and cuisines.

⑥ MIDDLE EAST: ARABIAN DESERT

Oases in the desert were some of our first orchards. Nomadic peoples tended the fruits grown there as they crossed the desert, moving from watering hole to watering hole.

⑦ SOUTH ASIA: BANANAS

Bananas are yellow, right? Think again! Only some bananas are yellow—others are red or blue!

⑧ THAILAND: ORCHIDS

Glorious orchids have some truly ingenious ways of attracting pollinators. Some flower forms are so specialized that they attract only one type of insect!

⑨ ISLANDS of SOUTHEAST ASIA

Extra pepper on your pasta? A sprinkle of cinnamon on your hot chocolate? Coffee anyone? Rain forest products touch our lives in so many unexpected ways.

CHERRY BLOSSOM, JAPAN

Every spring across Japan, millions of people celebrate *hanami*—the cherry blossom festival. Cherry trees bloom for only two weeks a year at any time from March to May. The timing depends on the weather. In spring, Japanese TV weather forecasts include a section called "the cherry blossom front," which gives details of when the blossoms are expected to appear.

Putting on a show
Cherry blossoms can be white, deep pink, and occasionally yellow.

Warbling white-eye (Zosterops japonicus)
The white-eyes feed on insects attracted by the cherry blossom nectar.

Urban beauties
Flowering cherry trees grow in most Japanese towns and cities.

Japan

Sika deer (Cervus nippon)
For a few weeks in spring, herds of sika deer gather beneath cherry blossom trees. They have learned that picnicking visitors will feed them.

Hanami started around 1,200 years ago. The first festivals probably paid tribute to the native Japanese cherry (*Cerasus jamasakura*) called *sakura*. Since then, more than 600 varieties have been developed. Flowering cherries are Japan's most important trees. Representations of cherry blossom are used in art, films, and literature.

During *hanami*, people gather under the cherry blossom to have picnics and parties. At night, paper lanterns are hung from the trees to allow visitors to view the flowers after dark. Most people visit the cherry trees at least once during *hanami*.

Brown eared bulbul
(*Hypsipetes amaurotis*)
The high-pitched squeaking call of the bulbul can be heard throughout springtime.

Saxaul tree (Haloxylon ammodendron)
This tree can be a lifesaver! It has a soft bark that acts like sponge and stores water. Thirsty voyagers can squeeze the bark and drink.

Shrubby sophora
(Sophora flavescens)
Scientists are researching the shrubby sophora as it contains unique chemicals that may treat heart disease.

Bindweed
(Convolvulus ammonia)
This is one of the few flowering plants in the Gobi Desert.

Gobi berry (Nitraria sibirica
Ripe Gobi berries are collected, dried, and stored for winter.

Binding bacterium
Black hair moss growing.

Tasty vegetable
Fat choy can be eaten.

Wiry food
Dried fat choy looks similar to wire wool.

Black hair moss
(Nostoc flagelliforme)
Black hair moss is a bacterium. Though not a plant, it is used as a vegetable called "fat choy" in Chinese cookery. Dried, it looks like wire wool. The moss is important in protecting the Gobi because it helps prevent soil erosion.

GOBI DESERT, CHINA and MONGOLIA

The Gobi Desert covers much of Mongolia and part of northern China. It is battered by strong winds, so in some areas, all soil and sand have been blown away and only bare rocks remain. In spring, there are giant yellow sandstorms. When the dust lands, it carpets the ground. As a result, the desert landscape is slowly extending.

Not all deserts are hot: some are extremely cold. Gobi temperatures can drop to −40°C (−40°F) at night. The word "desert" means a place where it does not often rain. There are parts of the Gobi where there has been no rainfall for many years. In most areas of the Earth, natural salts from underground rocks rise to the surface and are washed away by rain. But in the dry Gobi, they form thick crusts called salt deserts. Only a few specialized plants can survive in this remote habitat.

Wild leek (*Allium tricoccum*)
Bactrian camels are farmed for milk in the Gobi. Sometimes they eat so many wild leeks that the milk tastes like them.

Wild onion
(*Allium polyrhizum*)
Wild onions grow well in dry, rocky areas and can be eaten by people.

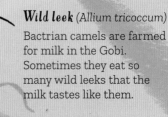

Tamarisk
(*Tamarix arceuthoides*)
Tamarisks grow on the banks of the few streams in the Gobi.

Goyo (*Cynomorium songaricum*)
Goyos contain no chlorophyll, so they cannot photosynthesize. Instead, they suck nutrients from the roots of other plants.

Desert broom-rape
(*Cistanche deserticola*)
Some people believe that the dried stems of this plant can improve human memory.

Juniper *(Juniperus communis)*

It was once believed that burning juniper branches would keep houses safe from witches.

Pallas' wallflower *(Erysimum pallasii)*

Wallflowers grow in extremely rocky places where they do not compete with other plants.

VIRGIN KOMI FOREST, RUSSIA

The spectacular Komi Forest is a UNESCO World Heritage Site and part of the Ural Mountains in northern Russia, on the border between Asia and Europe. Komi is a vast stretch of ancient forest largely unchanged by human activity. There are few roads through the woodland and Komi has very clean rivers and air. Plants can be damaged by pollution, but the lack of man-made chemicals here helps Komi keep its high biodiversity.

Winter temperatures can drop to −40°C (−40°F) and snow lies on the ground for around seven months a year. Dominant trees are mighty spruce, fir, and larch. Komi forms part of the boreal forest, which is the world's largest biome, or community of plants and animals living in a similar climate. Gold has been discovered beneath the Komi Forest. There are plans to begin mining that could involve cutting down trees and may threaten the health of the habitat.

Bird cherry
(Prunus padus)

The fruit tastes bitter to people but is enjoyed by birds.

Russian larch *(Larix sibirica)*

Pine trees produce a sticky liquid called resin that protects damaged bark against infection.

Blackcurrant
(Ribes nigrum)

Blackcurrants can be used to make a natural dye for fabrics, as well as being eaten.

Arctic sorrel *(Oxyria digyna)*

This was one of the first plants to grow after the glaciers melted at the end of the last Ice Age. Their 12,000-year-old pollen has been found in the mountains.

Fragile fern (*Cystopteris fragilis*)
This fern only grows in sheltered parts of the forest because the stem breaks easily.

Silver birch (*Betula pendula*)
Birch trees provide food for at least 500 species of insect.

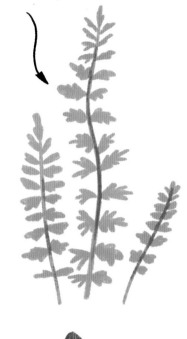

Arctic Ocean

Virgin Komi Forest

Russia

Fairy fingers (Clavaria fragilis)
The fruiting part of this fungus appears above ground for just a short time.

Arctic paintbrush (*Castilleja elegans*)
This plant is so called because its leaves look like artists' brushes dipped in paint.

Alpine woodsia (*Woodsia alpina*)
Also known as alpine cliff fern, these ferns are found across the world's Arctic regions.

Arctic cowslip (*Caltha palustris*)
This cowslip likes to grow in wet meadows.

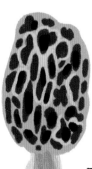

Morel (*Morchella esculenta*)
This is the same fungus that grows in Canada's Wood Buffalo Park. Some fungus species have spread to many parts of the world.

APPLES, KAZAKHSTAN

In the mountains of Kazakhstan grows an important tree species that is close to extinction —the wild apple (*Malus sieversii*). This tree looks familiar because it is the ancestor of most modern apples, which are grown all over the world.

Humans have been eating apples for at least 8,000 years. They were stored and transported far from the mountains to become one of our most widespread fruits. They have a place in many cultures, and we tell stories about them! They feature in fairy tales and in mythology—their name has even been adopted by one computer manufacturer!

Apple seeds almost always grow into a slightly changed form. That's why we have more than 7,000 known varieties today. Yet the origins of the apple you ate for lunch probably trace back to the forests of Kazakhstan, where the name of the former capital city, Almaty, means "full of apples."

Russia

Kazakhstan

Kyrgyzstan

Uzbekistan

Redwing (*Turdus iliacus*)
Fallen apples are an important food for migrating birds, such as redwings, that fly south.

Juicy fruits
Apples are around 85 percent water and are an excellent source of vitamin C.

Handle with care
Eating apples are often picked by hand to avoid bruising.

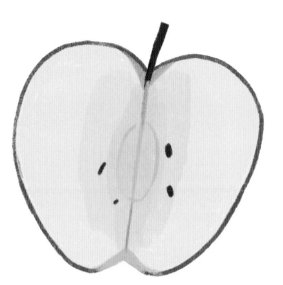

Brown bear (Ursus arctos)
Before their winter hibernation, bears feed on fallen fruit and disperse the seeds in their droppings.

Pollinated by bees
Most apple blossoms starts off pink and gradually change to white. Bees are the most important pollinators of apples.

Seeds of life
An average apple contains ten seeds.

Popular and delicious
First recognized in 1872, from 1968 to 2018, "Red Delicious" was the most popular apple variety grown in the USA.

Veratile and varied
Modern apples come in a wide range of textures and tastes. They also have many uses—they can be eaten raw, baked in pies, or squeezed into apple juice.

POMEGRANATES, TURKEY and the CAUCASUS

The pomegranate (*Punica granatum*) has a very special place in human culture. It is drought-tolerant and probably originated in the region around Iran. People gathered fruit from the spiny shrubs that grew wild. Then, about 5,000 years ago, we discovered how to grow and care for the long-lived trees, making them one of the very first fruits to be cultivated.

Pomegranates are known as *nar* in Turkish and are an important crop for many farmers. They are often seen as symbols of good luck. In Turkey and other Mediterranean countries, newlyweds break a pomegranate on their doorstep before entering their new house.

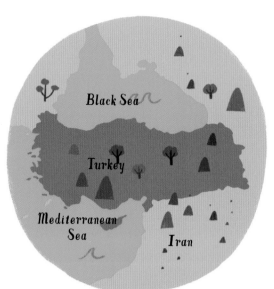

Bonsai pomegranate
Pomegranates are one of the most popular bonsai trees. Bonsai is the art of growing miniature trees.

Family farming
Most pomegranate trees are grown on family farms where everyone helps with the harvest.

Sacred trees
The pomegranate is one of the four sacred trees of Islam. It is said that a single seed from every fruit is holy and has spiritually cleansing effects if eaten.

Beautiful blooms

Pomegranate flowers are pollinated by bees. Some tree varieties do not produce fruit but are grown for their beautiful blossoms.

Super seedy

People once believed that all pomegranates contained exactly 613 seeds, but in fact it can be any number between 200 and 600.

Pomegranate molasses

When pomegranate juice is boiled, most of its water evaporates, leaving a sweet liquid called molasses. This is a popular ingredient in Middle Eastern cooking.

Good for the blood

Some experiments show that drinking pomegranate juice can reduce blood pressure.

Pomegranate in cooking

Pomegranate seeds are used as a spice called *anardana*. The juice and fruit are used in many types of dishes.

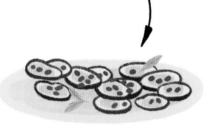

Eurasian magpie (*Pica pica*)
Rosy starling (*Pastor roseus*)

Magpies and rosy starlings open the tough skin on pomegranate fruit and eat the seeds inside.

Brown rat (*Rattus norvegicus*)

Brown rats often climb pomegranate trees to eat the fruit and can damage the crop.

Codling moth (*Cydia pomonella*)

Pomegranate leaves are the main food for growing caterpillars.

MIDDLE EAST, ARABIAN DESERT

The Arabian Desert is the largest desert in Asia. Here, the Sun rules and there is very little rain—temperatures vary from 50°C (122°F) to below freezing at night.

Part of this desert is a vast "erg"—an area of sand sculpted by the winds into hills called dunes. The plants that live in the erg most often grow in special places called oases. These form where underground springs or rivers rise to the surface. These watering places are regularly visited by migrating birds. Over time, the bird droppings help create fertile land in which crops can be planted. Today, a number of unique, hardy plants can be found in these extraordinary places.

Desert rose
(Adenium obesum)
The swollen trunks of the desert rose store water. Their sap is used as an arrow poison to help hunt animals in Africa.

Caper bush
(Capparis spinosa)
The buds and fruits of the caper bush can be salted or pickled and used as a seasoning.

Mediterranean Sea

Iraq

Egypt

Arabian Desert

Arabian Sea

Aloe vera
(Aloe vera)
Originating in the Arabian Peninsula, soothing gel from the leaves of aloe vera are used to treat sunburn.

Ghaf
(Prosopis cineraria)
The ghaf tree is fast-growing and an essential source of food, fuel, shelter, and medicine for people and animals living in the desert.

Salt bush (Seidlitzia stocksii)
The ash of the salt bush can be used instead of soap for cleaning clothes.

People and plants

Traditionally, dates are a very popular treat in Middle Eastern homes. Often arranged on silver dishes, they are served with hot, sweet tea. Now, delicious dates are eaten worldwide.

Lemon (*Citrus limon*)

Lemons are an excellent source of vitamin C.

Goat (*Capra hircus*)

Domestic goats are very much at home in the tough desert environment. Their droppings help fertilize crops and plants.

Apricot (*Prunus armeniaca*)

Wild apricot trees grow protected from the Sun in the shade of the taller date palms. Apricots can be eaten fresh or they can be dried to preserve them for longer.

Ring-necked parakeet (*Psittacula krameri*)

These bright parakeets feast on dates as they travel from oasis to oasis. They disperse seeds in their droppings as they go.

Date palm (*Phoenix dactylifera*)

Tall, deep-rooted date palms are at the heart of many oases. Their sweet fruits help feed the nomadic peoples of the desert and their livestock.

Myna bird (*Acridotheres tristis*)

Invasive common myna birds are relatively new residents of the oases where they thrive on a diet of fruit and insects.

81

BANANAS, SOUTH ASIA

Bananas do not grow on trees! They are very tall —sometimes 7.5 m (25 ft)—tree-like herbaceous perennials that do not have woody trunks. It takes each plant around a year to produce fruit and an average of six months to ripen before the plant dies. A few older varieties grow from seed. But in most cases, a new plant grows from the underground roots of the dead plant. These new suckers are called "pups."

Wild bananas originate in Asia but modern bananas grow on plantations and produce more and larger fruit with smaller seeds. This is because farmers have selectively bred varieties with these characteristics.

Bananas grow in bunches called "hands." They usually have between 10 and 20 individual bananas but one giant hand contained 473! Bananas are very slightly radioactive— though not sufficiently to make people ill. India produces more bananas than any other country.

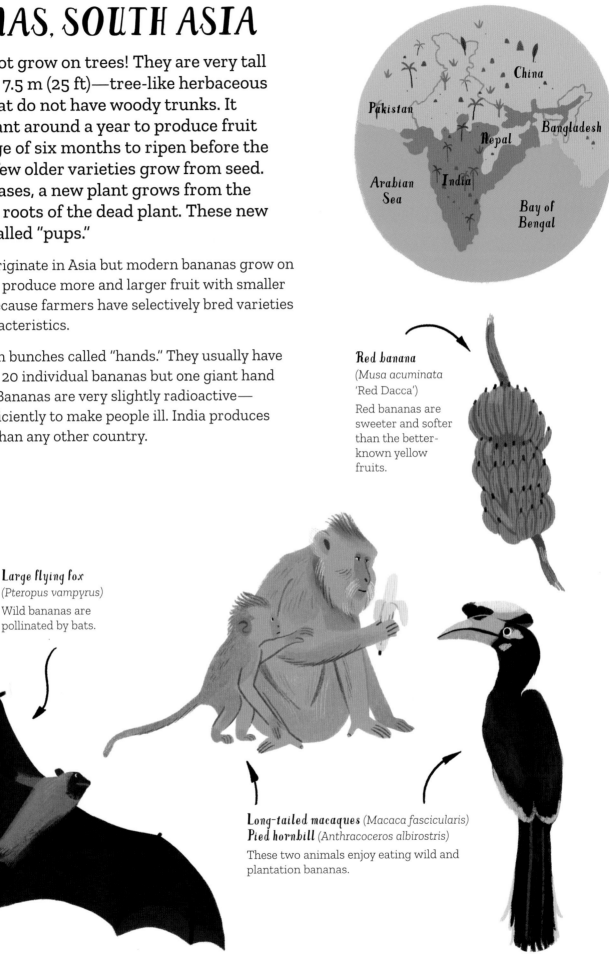

Red banana
(Musa acuminata 'Red Dacca')
Red bananas are sweeter and softer than the better-known yellow fruits.

Large flying fox
(Pteropus vampyrus)
Wild bananas are pollinated by bats.

Long-tailed macaques *(Macaca fascicularis)*
Pied hornbill *(Anthracoceros albirostris)*
These two animals enjoy eating wild and plantation bananas.

Gassy fruits

Ripe bananas produce a gas called ethylene that helps other fruits ripen.

Meaty flowers

Banana flowers are cooked and eaten as a substitute for meat.

Blue Java banana
(Musa acuminata)

This variety is called the "ice cream" banana because it has a strong taste that is very similar to vanilla.

Cavendish banana
(Musa acuminata)

The most popular banana in cultivation is the Cavendish variety. Production is currently threatened by a fungal disease that may mean an end to the Cavendish as we know them.

Praying hands

Sometimes bananas do not grow as separate fruit. Instead, they fuse together to form clumps. These are called "praying hands" bananas.

Banana leaf thatch

Waxy banana leaves are waterproof and make an excellent roof for nearby buildings.

ORCHIDS, THAILAND

Thailand is known as *Gluay Mhai*—"the land of the orchids." It is home to more than 1,500 species of wild orchid, and it is also the world's main producer of commercially farmed orchids.

There are more than 28,000 species of orchid worldwide. These clever plants have inventive ways of attracting pollinators. Some attract male insects by looking like female insects, some produce super-tempting sweet scents, while others reek of carrion to attract flies. Many are "epiphytes," or plants that grow on other plants. Some can be found up high in the rain forest canopy. Others grow on the ground.

Orchids produce little pollen packages to stick to pollinators. Some orchids are so specialized that they can only be pollinated by one species of insect! Many orchids have a specially adapted large petal that acts as a landing platform for pollinators. Orchids produce the smallest of all seeds—you can hold more than 100 million in one hand.

Medusa orchid
(Bulbophyllum medusae)
This orchid is named after Medusa from Greek mythology, whose hair was replaced by writhing snakes.

Tonsil orchid
(Vrydagzynea lancifolia)
Part of the flower of this orchid is shaped like the tonsils in the back of our throat.

Queen of the orchids
(Grammatophyllum speciosum)
This is world's largest orchid. It can reach 7.5 m (25 ft) tall!

Malaysian orchid
(Medinilla myriantha)
These orchids do not need soil to grow. They absorb water and nutrients through their leaves and roots.

Coconut orchid
(Maxillaria tenuifolia)
The flowers of this orchid have a strong coconut scent.

Helmet orchid
(Corybas carinatus)
This tiny, rare orchid attracts insect pollinators by looking like a fungus.

Orchid mantis
(Hymenopus coronatus)

The incredible orchid mantis is a hunter camouflaged to look like orchid petals! It ambushes insects that mistake it for a flower.

Orchid farming

Orchid farmers know the exact conditions required to produce perfect flowers.

Hand-pollinated vanilla orchid

Every vanilla orchid is pollinated by hand.

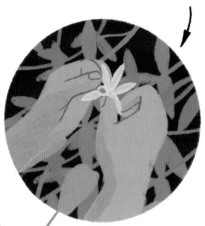

Dried vanilla pods

Imagine ice cream without vanilla! The dried pods add that special sugary,-floral hit.

Vanilla bean orchid
(Vanilla planifolia)

Vanilla comes from an orchid. The spice grows in long seed pods.

Floating markets

Thousands of orchids are sold every day at Thailand's beautiful floating markets.

ISLANDS of SOUTHEAST ASIA

There are more than 25,000 islands and small islets in Southeast Asia. Their lush rain forests are home to plants that are extremely useful to humans. Indigenous people have lived in Asian rain forests for thousands of years and have learned what plants are safe to use and how to find them. Timber, firewood, fruits, nuts, spices, and medicines are all found in this habitat. Dyes can be made from berries and textiles from plant strands. Some plants have many uses. For example, the coconut palm can give fruit, oil, water, rope, timber, and leaves for weaving.

We still learn from local knowledge and skill today. Every day, people around the world use items from the rain forest without realizing their origins. Indigenous people took small amounts of these products but more widespread harvesting can occur. As a result, rain forests are threatened by logging, palm oil plantations, and farming. Fortunately, many plant products are now grown sustainably on local farms.

Durian (*Durio zibethinus*)
Durian is the world's smelliest fruit! It has the scent of badly rotten eggs.

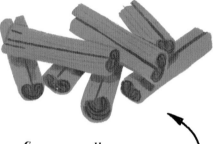

Cinnamon quills
Pieces of peeled and dried cinnamon bark are called "quills."

Orangutan
(*Pongo pygmaeus*)
Fresh durian is one of orangutans' best-loved foods.

Damaging deforestation
It takes just a few minutes to cut down a giant tree and 200 years for another to grow in its place.

Stripping the forest of nutrients
When logs are removed from the forest, life-giving nutrients are taken from the habitat.

Coffee beans

Ripe coffee (*Coffea*) beans are bright red.

Cinnamon
(Cinnamomum cassia)

Cinnamon spice, used in cooking and drinks, is the dried and crushed bark of the cinnamon tree.

Black pepper *(Piper nigrum)*

Black pepper is the world's most popular spice. It was once so valuable that it was used in place of money.

Ginger *(Zingiber officinale)*

Ginger plants are about 1 m (3 ft) tall. Only their thick, woody roots are used as a spice.

Oil palm tree *(Elaeis guineensis)*

Parts of the rain forest have been cut down in order to grow oil palm trees. Their fruits produce oil used in many everyday products and foods.

EUROPE

Think "Europe" and you might think historic cities and beautiful medieval buildings, but this continent also has some amazing wild areas where plants and animals can be found. There are mountains, rivers, regions of moderate weather, areas of cold winters, and others of hot summers. More of Europe's land is suitable for farming than in any other continent, and around 40 percent is used for agriculture.

In the north and northeast, there are conifer forests of fir, pine, spruce, and larch. Grassland lies in the southeast. In the Mediterranean areas, plants that enjoy a hot, dry climate—such as olive trees—can be found. Much of Europe was once covered by ancient forest, but now only fragments remain.

① BRITAIN and IRELAND: PEAT BOG

Mysterious peat bogs hide all kinds of secrets! There is sphagnum moss that can be used to dress wounds and more than one plant that likes to eat lunch while it is still wriggling or buzzing and very much alive!

② SWEDEN: PINE FOREST HABITAT

The conifer forests of Sweden are strangely quiet. A deep layer of pine needles softens sounds and is dotted with bright fungi and flowers.

③ WESTERN EUROPE: COMMON OAK

From the smallest of acorns, these huge, long-lived oaks grow. Oaks are home to more species than any other European tree.

④ SPAIN and PORTUGAL: SCRUBLAND

Mediterranean scrubland is alive with many of the tastes and scents we enjoy every day: sage, rosemary, and lavender. You can also find mysterious mandrakes here!

⑤ SWITZERLAND: SWISS NATIONAL PARK

Small, low-growing and very, very tough, alpine plants have a delicacy that defies the cold, windy, and exposed environment in which they grow.

Snow gentian
(Gentiana nivalis)

Fern leaf peony
(Paeonia tenuifolia)

Sweet chestnut
(Castanea sativa)

Scots pine
(Pinus sylvestris)

Stemless gentian
(Gentiana acaulis)

Fly agaric
(Amanita muscaria)

Common oak
(Quercus robur)

Ragged robin
(Silene flos-cuculi)

Round-leaved sundew
(Drosera rotundifolia)

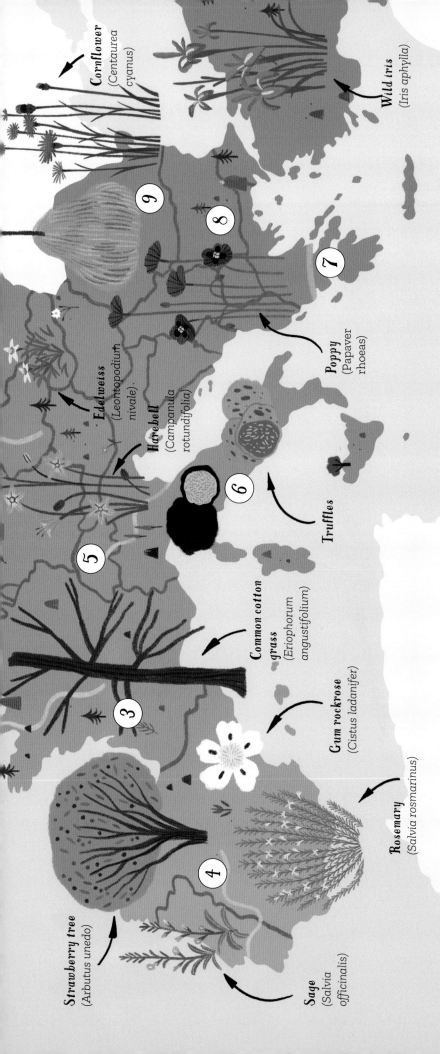

Cornflower
(*Centaurea cyanus*).

Wild iris
(*Iris aphylla*)

Strawberry tree
(*Arbutus unedo*)

Edelweiss
(*Leontopodium nivale*).

Harebell
(*Campanula rotundifolia*)

Poppy
(*Papaver rhoeas*)

Common cotton grass
(*Eriophorum angustifolium*)

Gum rockrose
(*Cistus ladanifer*)

Truffles

Sage
(*Salvia officinalis*)

Rosemary
(*Salvia rosmarinus*)

⑨ ⑧ ⑦ ⑤ ⑥ ③ ④

There are regions of Europe, such as the hay meadows of Romania, where traditional farming practices can be found. These work in greater harmony with the natural world, leaving space for wild plants and animals to thrive. Oak and conifer forests also offer space for wildlife. Many oaks are older than some of Europe's legendary castles!

Europe's ancient and mysterious bogs are one of the world's most threatened habitats. They take thousands of years to form, and if we destroy them, their plants will vanish forever.

From wetlands to the high meadows of the Alps, fertile Europe is full of surprises. Here you can hunt truffles in Italy, taste olives in Greece, and forage for wild herbs in Spain and Portugal.

⑦ **GREECE: OLIVES**
One of the first trees to be cultivated for their fruit, olives contain an oil that has been central to human health since the Bronze Age.

⑨ **ROMANIA: MEADOWS**
Traditionally managed hay meadows buzz with bees and other pollinators. They feast on herbs growing among the grass and, in their turn, provide food for other animals.

⑥ **ITALY: TRUFFLES**
Sometimes referred to as "black gold," truffles are some of the most expensive foods in the world. But they begin life in the forest, hidden deep in the earth.

⑧ **BULGARIA: VERGES**
Bulgaria's protected grass verges explode with roadside plants and flowers. These areas form a huge patchwork of habitats that attract pollinators and help keep the ecosystems healthy.

BRITAIN and IRELAND, PEAT BOG

Peatland bogs—like Fenn's, Whixall, and Bettisfield Mosses National Nature Reserve—are mysterious places that preserve the past. Peat is formed by decomposing plants, often mosses, that died more than 10,000 years ago. A bog is the soft, spongy wetland where layers of peat form.

Bogs are threatened habitats and occur only occasionally. They begin in poorly drained wet ground. When plants die in water, rather than rot away, they sink and disintegrate. Every year, more plants grow and die, building up layers that can be 10 m (25 ft) deep.

Peatland holds water like a sponge, is low in nutrients and oxygen, and the dead plants make the habitat slightly acidic. Only specialized plants can thrive here. For hundreds of years, peat was cut, dried, and used as fuel called turf. The same conditions that prevent plants from fully decomposing also prevent other things from decaying. Ancient weapons, tools, and even bodies have been discovered in bogs.

Ragged robin
(*Silene flos-cuculi*)
Ragged robins are one of the main nectar plants for insects around the bog.

Common hawker dragonfly (*Aeshna juncea*)
Peatland specialists, hawkers hunt for butterflies and other insects that visit to drink or feed on the plants.

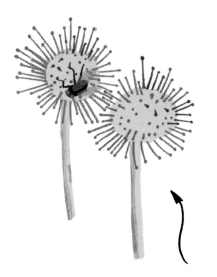

Round-leaved sundew (*Drosera rotundifolia*)
Delicate sundews hide a grisly secret. They have a taste for live prey! Every leaf is covered with gluey droplets that trap visiting insects. The sundew's leaf curls around the insect and the plant slowly digests its prey.

Sphagnum moss
(*Sphagnum flexuosum*)
The most common inhabitant of the bog, this moss can hold up to 20 times its own weight of water.

Bog myrtle *(Myrica gale)*
Visitors to bog habitats often carry bog myrtle leaves. The strong, sweet smell keeps away mosquitos.

Bog asphodel
(Narthecium ossifragum)
"Ossifragum" means "bone-breaker." It was thought that if sheep ate asphodels then their legs would become weak and break. Happily, this is not the case!

Bogbean
(Menyanthes trifoliata)
Their leaves look exactly like the leaves of fava beans, hence the name.

Grass snake *(Natrix natrix)*
Grass snakes are non-venomous hunters that feed on the bogs' frogs.

Bladderwort
(Utricularia vulgaris)
Bladderwort is a super-fast killer! It floats on water waiting for prey to brush against the trigger hairs of the trapdoor of its "bladder." The door snaps open and the insect is sucked in. Each snap takes 10–15 thousandths of a second.

Common cotton grass
(Eriophorum angustifolium)
The fluffy seed heads of cotton grass were once used to fill pillows.

Bog rosemary *(Andromeda polifolia)*
Bog rosemary has leaves that are green on top and white underneath.

KOLMÅRDEN PINE FOREST, SWEDEN

Sweden is a land of rich forests, lakes, and islands. Trees cover nearly 70 percent of the country. They include deciduous species like birch and alder, but it is the conifers that dominate the forests. Norway spruce and Scots pine trees probably evolved in this landscape.

Kolmården is an ancient forest on the coast. Trees in north Sweden are not used for timber, and are called "natural forests." Only trees in the south are harvested commercially. Sweden keeps its forests healthy by planting saplings to replace cut trees. It was one of the first countries to pass laws protecting the forests.

Much of the Kolmården forest is a nature reserve for wildlife and people. The forests are quiet and full of shadows, with a thick layer of soft pine needles underfoot. There are many open areas where plants photosynthesize and grow. The butterflies and bees live here—they are the heart of the forest's biodiversity.

Heather (*Calluna vulgaris*)

Heather is the main food for willow grouse (*Lagopus lagopus*), one of the forest's most widespread birds.

Scots pine
(*Pinus sylvestris*)

These are the only pine trees that are native to northern Europe.

Fly agaric
(*Amanita muscaria*)

The toadstools of fairy tales! These fungi can cause people and other animals to hallucinate.

Wild angelica
(*Angelica archangelica*)

Wild angelica grows to a height of 2.5 m (8 ft). Traditionally, the stem was eaten as a vegetable that could be stored for use in winter.

Norwegian Sea

Norway

North Sea

Finland

Sweden

Kolmården

Baltic Sea

Wolf's bane
(Aconitum lycoctonum)
Wolf's bane is extremely poisonous. It was once used to tip the arrows of hunters seeking wolves.

Whorled Solomon's-seal
(Polygonatum verticillatum)
This likes to grow on the steep sides of wooded gorges.

Spiked speedwell
(Veronica spicata)
The deep violet-blue flowers really zing out at dusk.

Wood anemone
(Anemonoides nemorosa)
Wood anemones are one of the first flowers to open at the end of winter.

Snow gentian *(Gentiana nivalis)*
The blue flowers only open when the Sun is shining and the temperature is higher than 10°C (50 °F).

Acorns young and old

Young acorns are green and sit inside a small cup. Ripe acorns turn brown and drop from the cup to the floor below.

Ancient oak tree

Oaks trees can live more than 1,000 years and are often given names such as the Chapel Oak in France, which has a small church inside the huge trunk.

Beefsteak fungus

(Fistulina hepatica)

Beefsteak fungus looks just like a slab of uncooked meat. It even "bleeds" drops of red juice when it is cut open.

COMMON OAK, WESTERN EUROPE

Oaks (*Quercus robur*) are deciduous trees that drop their leaves every year. They are widespread throughout western Europe, and are home to the highest biodiversity of any European tree. They provide food and shelter to more than 2,000 other species of wildlife. The floor of oak woodland hosts an impressive variety of plants. They thrive because oak trees do not have a dense canopy, which means there are gaps between the leaves that allow sunlight to pass through.

A single oak can have 250,000 leaves that decay over winter and provide perfect nourishment for flowers to use the following spring. Most blooms open before the oak leaves grow so they can be at their best in full sunlight. Each oak produces thousands of seeds called acorns, almost all of which are eaten by birds and mammals. But if just one acorn every century manages to grow into a mature tree, then the forest will continue into the future.

Leafy incubator

Female oak gall wasps (*Cynips quercusfolii*) lay one egg into an oak-leaf bud. This creates a small ball that looks like fruit but is really a shell to protect the grub that is growing inside.

Oak processionary moth
(*Thaumetopoea processionea*)

More than 100 caterpillars walk along branches in nose-to-tail lines hunting for fresh oak leaves to eat.

Growth rings

Inside an oak's trunk there are growth rings. Each one represents one year of life. Counting the rings gives the tree's exact age.

Oak flowers

Each tree has both female and male flowers. Male flowers are long, dangly clusters, and female flowers look like tiny red buds hidden at the bottom of leaves.

The United Kingdom

The Netherlands

Belgium

Germany

France

Switzerland Austria

Spain

Italy

Jay (*Garrulus glandarius*)

Jays cache ripe acorns in the ground. The forgotten ones grow into new oak trees.

Bay of Biscay

Spain

Portugal

Mediterranean Sea

Mandrake (*Mandragora officinarum*)
Superstition and magic surrounds harvesting the mandrake, the roots of which are thought to look like a human. When the mandrake is pulled out of the ground it is thought to scream. And it is said that anyone hearing the scream will die!

Strawberry tree (*Arbutus unedo*)
The fruit of these trees look like strawberries, but they are not a related species. Strawberry trees are part of the heather family.

Naked man orchid
(*Orchis italica*)
The lip of the naked man orchid looks exactly like a man wearing no clothes!

Hoop petticoat daffodil
(*Narcissus bulbocodium*)
These flowers have a wide, funnel-shaped flower that looks just like an old-fashioned skirt.

Paperwhite narcissus
(*Narcissus papyraceus*)
The scent of paperwhites is glorious! We now grow them indoors in pots to brighten the winter months.

Sage
(*Salvia officinalis*)
Sage isn't all about stuffing! It was once seen as a lucky plant that was carried to keep away evil spirits.

SCRUBLAND, SPAIN and PORTUGAL

The stony soil around the Mediterranean has produced some of our most delicious herbs. Every day, we eat them on pizzas and in stews and salads. Many of the herbs come from scrubland, a habitat called maquis that has hot, dry summers and mild winters.

Trees do not grow well in the poor maquis soil. This is a landscape of shrubs—low-growing plants with tough woody stems that are often evergreen. Most flowers bloom here in spring, as they need to be pollinated before the hot summer. Leaves are generally small so they do not absorb too much heat from the Sun and dry out. Most plants also contain oils that help stop them from burning. On late afternoons in summer, the air in the Algarve in Portugal carries a soft, sweet, floral fragrance. The wind mixes the scents of natural plant oils— including rosemary, myrtle, sage, thyme, and eucalyptus.

Rosemary *(Salvia rosmarinus)*
This aromatic herb was added to roasting meat at least 7,000 years ago.

Gum rockrose
(Cistus ladanifer)
Gum rockroses produce large amounts of highly flammable resin. In very hot weather, the plants can sometimes suddenly burst into flames.

Lavender *(Lavandula angustifolia)*
Lovely lavender oil has a soothing scent. Clothes are often stored with dried lavender sachets. The scent keeps away moths that lay eggs on wool. It is their caterpillars that nibble clothes.

Navelwort
(Umbilicus rupestris)
Navelwort grows best among stones. It sends out long roots in all directions to find water underground.

Wild cabbage
(Brassica oleracea)
This is the wild ancestor of food plants such as cauliflower, cabbage, and broccoli.

SWISS NATIONAL PARK, SWITZERLAND

The Swiss National Park combines jagged mountains, forests, and alpine meadows. It is a protected wilderness area studied by scientists and it is home to many unique species of plants and animals.

Spring arrives late in the Alps and summer is short, so plants need to reproduce quickly. Many flower at the same time, creating one of the most amazing sights in the mountains: the alpine meadow.

The meadows grow at the lower altitudes and are blanketed with bright blooms, each competing to attract pollinating insects. The soil in the Alps is frequently washed away with the melting snow and lacks nutrition.

Alpine flowers tend to be low-growing, which means they are able to withstand intense cold, wind, snow, and ice and can cope with ultraviolet radiation from the strong sunlight. Here, there are sedges and clump-forming grasses. Mosses, lichens, and mat-forming "cushion" plants are common, as they hug the ground and avoid the worst of the weather.

Globe flower
(Trollius europaeus)

Globe flowers need damp soil. They often grow next to mountain streams that bring clean water from the high peaks.

Harebell (Campanula rotundifolia)

The papery petals of harebells look delicate, but they can survive in high, exposed places, where their flexible stems bend in strong winds instead of breaking.

Alpine poppy (Papaver alpinum)

Cunningly, these poppies have a sweet scent but do not produce nectar. Visiting insects carry away pollen but do not get food as a reward.

Edelweiss (*Leontopodium nivale*)
This is the superstar of the Alps! Its yellow flowers are surrounded by woolly, white, star-shaped bracts. It lives in hard-to-reach places and was given as a symbol of love.

Alpine rock-jasmine
(*Androsace alpine*)
Flowers can be pink or white. Sometimes both tones exist on the same plant.

Stemless gentian (*Gentiana acaulis*)
True blue, these short-stemmed trumpet flowers grow together as a cushion or mat.

Michaelmas daisy
(*Aster amellus*)
These daises are one of the tallest flowers in the Alps.

Glacier buttercup
(*Ranunculus glacialis*)
Glacier buttercups grow at higher altitudes than almost any other Alpine plant.

TRUFFLES, ITALY

Hidden deep in the earth among the roots of oak, hazel, and cherry trees, there are strange fungi that look a little like small potatoes. These are truffles (*Tuber melanosporum*), one of the world's sought-after delicacies. They have an aroma and taste that is difficult to describe, and that science has not yet analyzed fully. It is a little garlicky, nutty, and earthy.

Truffles are the fruiting body of an underground fungus that spreads throughout the woodland. Fruiting bodies contain spores, a kind of seed, that is dispersed by animals. Truffle fungi take valuable sugars from nearby tree roots. In exchange, they contribute small amounts of nutrients, such as iron and copper, that the tree needs to stay healthy but cannot easily take from the soil.

Because truffles are scarce and form underground, they are very difficult to find. Professional truffle hunters keep the location of their hunting grounds a closely guarded secret.

Truffle pig
Pigs have an excellent sense of smell and are sometimes used to find truffles.

Truffle oil

Olive oil can be infused with a little truffle. The tasty oil can then be drizzled over salads and pasta dishes.

Switzerland

France

Italy

Corsica

Sardinia

Packed with spores

Each truffle contains millions of tiny spores.

Black truffles

Black truffles grow among the roots of deciduous trees and are gathered to be eaten or sold.

Traditional Italian truffle dog

Hunters use specially trained dogs to sniff out truffles. The best-known Italian truffle-hunting breed is the curly coated Lagotto Romagnolo.

White gold!

In 2021, white truffles sold at £5,000 (US$6,800) a kilo (2.2lbs).

Leopard moth (Zeuzera pyrina)

Adult leopard moths search for olive groves in summer. This is where females lay their eggs. The caterpillars eat olive wood. They live inside the tree trunks and branches for up to three years before changing into adults.

Kalamata olives
(Olea europaea 'Kalamon')

This purple, shiny-skinned fruit is crowned the "queen of olives."

Healthy oil

Some 90 percent of olive trees are grown for oil production. Olive oil is one of the most nutritious of all oils.

Olive
(Olea europaea)

Blackcap (Sylvia atricapilla)

Blackcaps eat insects most of the year but feed on ripe olives in late summer.

Wild chrysanthemum
(Glebionis coronarium)

Fresh chrysanthemum leaves are used as a vegetable in the spring.

Death cap fungus
(Amanita phalloides)

Death cap fungus lives beneath olive trees and is deadly poisonous.

Chamomile (Chamaemelum nobile)

Dried chamomile flowers are used to make a soothing tea to aid digestion.

OLIVE GROVES, GREECE

People have had a taste for energy-packed olives since at least the Bronze Age. Olives and their oil are some of the most important ingredients in Mediterranean cooking and the oil is also used in cosmetics and as fuel for lamps.

Olive trees need warmth and plenty of sunshine to thrive and are cultivated in groves. The groves provide a home to many species of herbaceous plants and attract large numbers of insects and birds. The fruits are harvested in early winter when they are plump with oil. They are first washed and then ground to a pulp by heavy millstones. Next, a powerful press squeezes the pulp until it releases its valuable oil. The basic technique has changed very little in the last 5,000 years.

Every part of the long-lived tree helps people. Olive wood is used for indoor furniture and kitchenware. Even the leaves are made into a medicinal tea.

Turkey

Greece

Cyprus

Mediterranean Sea

Aegean Sea

Ionian Sea

All kinds of olives

There are many types of olive, each with its own taste, texture, size, and skin shade. Different regions of Greece specialize in certain varieties.

Poppy
(Papaver rhoeas)

Poppies are grown for their tiny black seeds, which are added to olive bread.

Bear's breeches (Acanthus mollis)

Bear's breeches are the national flower of Greece.

Saffron crocus (Crocus sativus)

These crocuses are cultivated to produce saffron, the world's most expensive spice. They are now being grown experimentally alongside olives as farmers diversify their crops.

Canterbury bells
(Campanula medium)

Canterbury bells grow in the shade of olive trees and encourage insects to pollinate the olive blossom.

ROADSIDE VERGES, BULGARIA

Bulgaria contains an impressive variety of habitats and is one of the most biodiverse countries in Europe. Much of the country is mountainous, but there are also rich grasslands and lush forests. It has a coastline on the west side of the Black Sea. The wild Bulgarian countryside is home to many of Europe's big predators, such as wolves, lynx, jackals, and bears—species that have disappeared from much of Europe.

As with many other countries, roadside verges have become one of the most important plant habitats. When not mown, grazed, or sprayed with pesticide, verges form long, thin nature reserves that cover huge distances. Many have been undisturbed for centuries and provide an ideal environment for the 170 plant species that are unique to Bulgaria. The climate is changeable and somewhat varied, with significant winter snowfall.

The Balkans

Black Sea

Bulgaria

Aegean Sea

Turkey

Date-plum *(Diospyros lotus)*
Delicious date-plums are neither dates nor plums but taste a little like both!

Sweet chestnut
(Castanea sativa)
Sweet chestnut trees are approximately 20 years old before they produce nuts.

Garbanzo (chickpea)
(Cicer arietinum)
Garbanzo seeds are very high in protein.

Winter aconite
(Eranthis hyemalis)
Yellow aconites are one of the first flowers to appear in spring.

Fern leaf peony
(Paeonia tenuifolia)
This plant has leaves that look like huge bunches of hair.

Solomon's lily
(Arum palaestinum)
Solomon's lily is one of the world's few purple-black flowers.

Fragrant hellebore
(Helleborus odorus)
Unlike most hellebores, the fragrant hellebore has a delicate, sweet smell.

Tulip
(Tulipa orphanidea)
The word tulip means "turban" and describes the shape of the flower before it opens.

Golden dog's tail *(Lamarckia aurea)*
This grass has a seed head that looks just like the shaggy tail of a dog!

Giant pink *(Dianthus giganteus)*
Each tall stem of a giant pink produces many flower heads.

MEADOWS, ROMANIA

Early summer in Romania is the best time and place to see traditional European hay meadows. Cows feed on grass in the summer. In winter, they are moved indoors and are fed on hay. Hay is grass and other herbs that are dried and stored to provide food for grazing animals. Each cow eats about 3.6 tonnes (4 tons) of hay between October and May so the farmers need to build up a substantial store.

Meadows grown for hay are not grazed. They are also not treated by pesticides or other chemicals. For this reason, pollinating insects thrive in the meadows. A wonderful mix of pink, yellow, blue, and red wild flowers bloom here until late summer when the grass is cut and dried in neat haystacks. This gives the flowers time to produce seeds that will be ready to grow the following year. About 300 years ago, meadows were commonplace in the countryside across the continent.

Fallow deer (Dama dama)
Fallow deer often visit the meadows to feed on the rich grass.

Snapdragon (Antirrhinum majus)
When the flower is squeezed, it opens up like the mouth of a mythical dragon and snaps shut when it is released. The seed head looks like a human skull!

Cornflower (Centaurea cyanus)
Cornflowers were once common among cereal crops, but changes in agriculture mean that these flowers are increasingly rare.

Peacock butterfly (Aglais io) **feeding on shaggy hawkweed** (Hieracium villosum)
The hay meadows are one of the most important feeding grounds for insects such as peacock butterflies.

Yellow rattle (Rhinanthus minor)
The seeds of this wildflower grow in small, hard pods. When they are ripe, the pods rattle in the wind.

Castle Bran
Castle Bran is the traditional home of Count Dracula and overlooks some of the hay meadows.

Dog's tooth violet
(Erythronium dens-canis)

Dog's tooth violets grow on the edges of the hay meadows, usually in the shade of a tree.

White stork *(Ciconia ciconia)*
White storks hunt in the long grass looking for insects and small animals.

Wild iris *(Iris aphylla)*
Wild irises are endangered over much of Europe. The Romanian hay meadows are one of their strongholds.

Unique haystacks
Romanian haystacks have a shape that is not seen in any other country.

Ukraine

Moldova

Romania

Black Sea

Bulgaria

Aegean Sea

Wild peonies
(Paeonia peregrina)

Each peony flower can be up to 13 cm (5 in) across.

Orange hawkweed
(Pilosella aurantiaca)

It was once believed that hawks regularly ate this weed to improve their eyesight.

107

Mountain avens
(Dryas octopetala)

White arctic heather
(Cassiope tetragona)

Jade vine
(Strongylodon
macrobotrys)

Arctic lupine
(Lupinus arcticus)

Labrador tea
(Rhododendron
groenlandicum)

OCEANIA

Located largely in the Southern Hemisphere, where winter begins in June, Oceania lies mostly to the southeast of Asia. It includes Australia, New Zealand, and many surrounding island countries. Some of these islands are volcanic—they rose up from the ocean bed during eruptions. Others are made of coral reefs, which are the hard skeletons of tiny marine creatures. Oceania is remote, varied, and home to more domestic sheep than to people!

Much of Oceania is desert but there are also areas of lush vegetation. How did these areas come to be so green? Some island plants originally arrived from Asia, their floating seeds

Rafflesia
(Rafflesia arnoldii)

carried by the powerful North Pacific Current. Ferns have no problem crossing open water. They reproduce through tiny spores, and can be blown hundreds of miles by strong winds. Just a few spores are enough to create a new colony of plants. Australia was once connected to India and Africa. When it broke away, it already had a wealth of plant life. Over millions of years, these have evolved to produce the unique species that live there today.

The Pacific Ocean, which surrounds Oceania, extends to the north and south polar regions. Although the Arctic can be challenging for plant life, it is connected by land to less harsh habitats. Some species have moved up from warmer landscapes farther south, slowly adapting to suit the new conditions. That is impossible in the Antarctic, which is why this coldest of all continents is home to only two species of flowering plant!

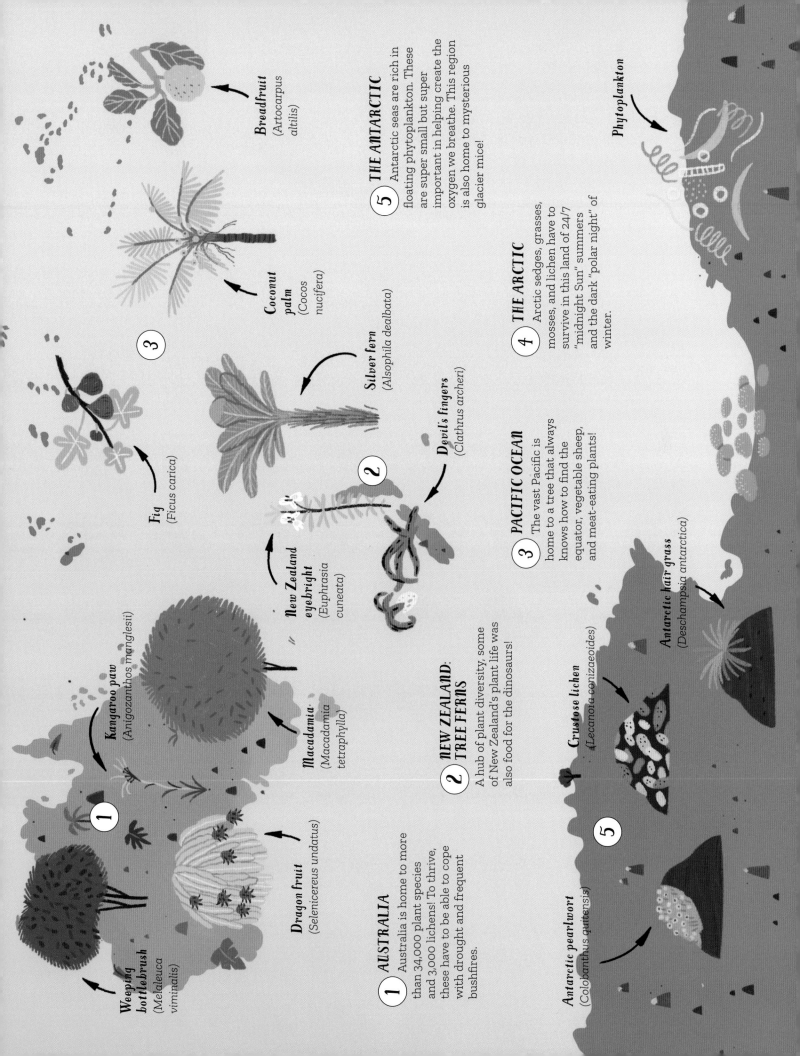

Breadfruit
(*Artocarpus altilis*)

(5) THE ANTARCTIC
Antarctic seas are rich in floating phytoplankton. These are super small but super important in helping create the oxygen we breathe. This region is also home to mysterious glacier mice!

Phytoplankton

Coconut palm
(*Cocos nucifera*)

Fig
(*Ficus carica*)

(3)

Silver fern
(*Alsophila dealbata*)

Devil's fingers
(*Clathrus archeri*)

(2)

New Zealand eyebright
(*Euphrasia cuneata*)

(4) THE ARCTIC
Arctic sedges, grasses, mosses, and lichen have to survive in this land of 24/7 "midnight Sun" summers and the dark "polar night" of winter.

(3) PACIFIC OCEAN
The vast Pacific is home to a tree that always knows how to find the equator, vegetable sheep, and meat-eating plants!

Kangaroo paw
(*Anigozanthos manglesii*)

Macadamia
(*Macadamia tetraphylla*)

(2) NEW ZEALAND: TREE FERNS
A hub of plant diversity, some of New Zealand's plant life was also food for the dinosaurs!

Dragon fruit
(*Selenicereus undatus*)

(1)

Weeping bottlebrush
(*Melaleuca viminalis*)

Crustose lichen
(*Lecanora conizaeoides*)

Antarctic hair grass
(*Deschampsia antarctica*)

(1) AUSTRALIA
Australia is home to more than 34,000 plant species and 3,000 lichens! To thrive, these have to be able to cope with drought and frequent bushfires.

Antarctic pearlwort
(*Colobanthus quitensis*)

(5)

AUSTRALIA

Australia broke away from other continents approximately 45 million years ago. Plants and animals already existed on the land, but over time they evolved some very different characteristics to other species around the world. Australia is the smallest of all the continents and is home to a collection of plants that do not exist anywhere else.

Australia has rich grasslands, eucalyptus woodlands, and the world's oldest rain forest, in Northern Queensland. But the country's biggest habitat is dry scrubland, a sandy landscape with poor soil, where summers are long, hot, and dry. Many scrubland plants stop growing and drop their leaves in the hottest weather, leaving stems and

Weeping bottlebrush
(*Melaleuca viminalis*)
Bottlebrushes are thirsty plants that like to grow close to streams or pools.

Moojar (*Nuytsia floribunda*)
The moojar's yellow flowers appear in December, giving it the name of the "Christmas tree."

Sandpaper wattle
(*Acacia denticulosa*)
This wattles' leaves are covered in tiny, sharp bumps that feel like sandpaper.

Pink mulla mulla
(*Ptilotus exaltatus*)
Mulla mullas usually flower immediately after a heavy rain.

branches only above ground. Because plants lose water through tiny holes in their leaves, dropping them stops the rest of the plant drying out and helps it to survive.

Low-growing scrubland plants are the main food for Australia's wallabies, kangaroos and wild camels.

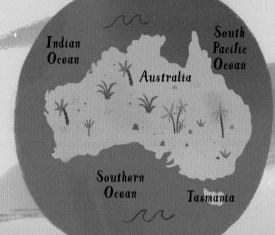

Indian Ocean

South Pacific Ocean

Australia

Southern Ocean

Tasmania

Bush nuts
Macadamia nuts are high in fat and are an important source of food for people and animals alike.

Dragon fruit *(Selenicereus undatus)*
Dragon fruit trees were grown on farms, but birds carried their seeds into wild areas and they can now be found in many dry landscapes.

Macadamia
(Macadamia tetraphylla)
Although macadamia nut trees are grown in hot countries around the world, they are an endangered species in their native Australia.

Kangaroo paw
(Anigozanthos manglesii)
When fully open, kangaroo paw flowers look exactly like the front foot and toes of a kangaroo!

Lantern banksia
(Banksia ericifolia)
Lantern banksia flowers produce so much nectar that it was once consumed by humans.

Grass tree *(Xanthorrhoea semiplana)*
The flowering stalk of this plant was used as the handle of a spear by Aboriginal peoples. A sharp wooden spearhead was fixed to the end.

Tasman Sea

New Zealand

South Pacific Ocean

Large-leaved kowhai
(Sophora tetraptera)
The tree ferns share their habitat with flowering plants like the kowhai.

Southern rātā
(Metrosideros umbellata)
New Zealand's prized rātā honey comes from these nectar-rich trees. The trees flower every couple of years.

Silver fern
(Alsophila dealbata)
Silver fern fronds are green on top and a beautiful silvery-white on the underside.

Kangaroo apple
(Solanum aviculare)
Ripe kangaroo apples are orange and very tasty, but unripe fruit is green and poisonous.

New Zealand eyebright
(Euphrasia cuneata)
Crushed eyebright flowers were once added to water and used to treat eye infections.

Fern spores
Each spore is a single cell. They grow in "sori," small brown structures, on the underside of fronds. They are dispersed by the wind.

Soft tree fern (*Cyathea smithii*)
These ferns need lots of moisture. Direct sunlight or even strong winds will dry out the plant and eventually kill it.

Natural art
Fern fiddlehead designs are important in Māori art. The spiral shape is called a *koru* and appears in many forms across New Zealand.

All curled up
New fern fronds start by uncoiling from a curled spiral called a fiddlehead.

Umbrella fern (*Sticherus cunninghamii*)
These drooping fronds form a dome "umbrella" shape and give the plant its name.

TREE FERNS, NEW ZEALAND

Tree ferns are not trees, despite having a trunk-like central stem. They first appeared around 300 million years ago and provided food for herbivore dinosaurs, like Diplodocus. Today, there are more than 12,000 living fern species, and they grow best in damp, cool locations.

Tree ferns have massive leaves that form a dense canopy in the understory of New Zealand's forests. Fern leaves are feathered and divided into many different shapes called fronds that grow from the central crown. Mature fern stems can be ecosystems in themselves—home to mosses, lichens, and other seedlings.

Tough and resilient, tree ferns are often the first to regrow after a bushfire. Ferns are nonflowering plants than do not produce seeds. Instead, they reproduce using spores. Spores grow on the underside of a frond. Fossil fuels we use today, such as oil and coal, are made from the compressed remains of ancient tree fern forests.

Hound's tongue fern (*Zealandia pustulata*)
Hound's tongue ferns are now popular houseplants all around the world.

Devil's fingers (*Clathrus archeri*)
Stinky devil's fingers fungus looks like a long-dead hand coming out of the soil. They have a truly revolting smell.

PACIFIC OCEAN

The Pacific Ocean is huge! It covers almost one third of the surface of the Earth; an area larger than all of Earth's land combined. Everything about the Pacific is extreme. It contains half of all the world's seawater and is deeper than any other ocean. The seabed inside the Mariana Trench is the lowest point on the planet, situated 10,984 m (36,037 ft) below sea level. It is home to more than 25,000 islands, reaching from the tropics to both polar regions.

Some vegetation has been transported between the various islands, but many other plants remain isolated because they are too far from any other islands to reach new habitats.

The Pacific Ocean is the original home of the amazing coconut palm, which is probably the most useful tree in the world. In fact, in the Sanskrit language, it is called *kalpa vriksha*—"the tree which provides all of life's necessities."

Fig (*Ficus carica*)
Fig seeds are often dispersed in the droppings of fruit bats.

Coconut palm (*Cocos nucifera*)
Coconut palms grow on most warm Pacific islands. They provide building materials, food, cosmetics, and wine.

Pitcher plant (*Nepenthes truncate*)
Meat-eating plants? Yes! Carnivorous pitcher plants attract, trap, and digest insects and small animals.

Breadfruit (*Artocarpus altilis*)
Cooked breadfruit tastes like fresh bread and is an important food for people living around the Pacific. Each tree can produce 200 kg (450 lb) of fruit a year.

Bakong (*Pandanus dubius*)
The bakong has hard, tough leaves that can be woven into mats. Its seeds taste like coconut.

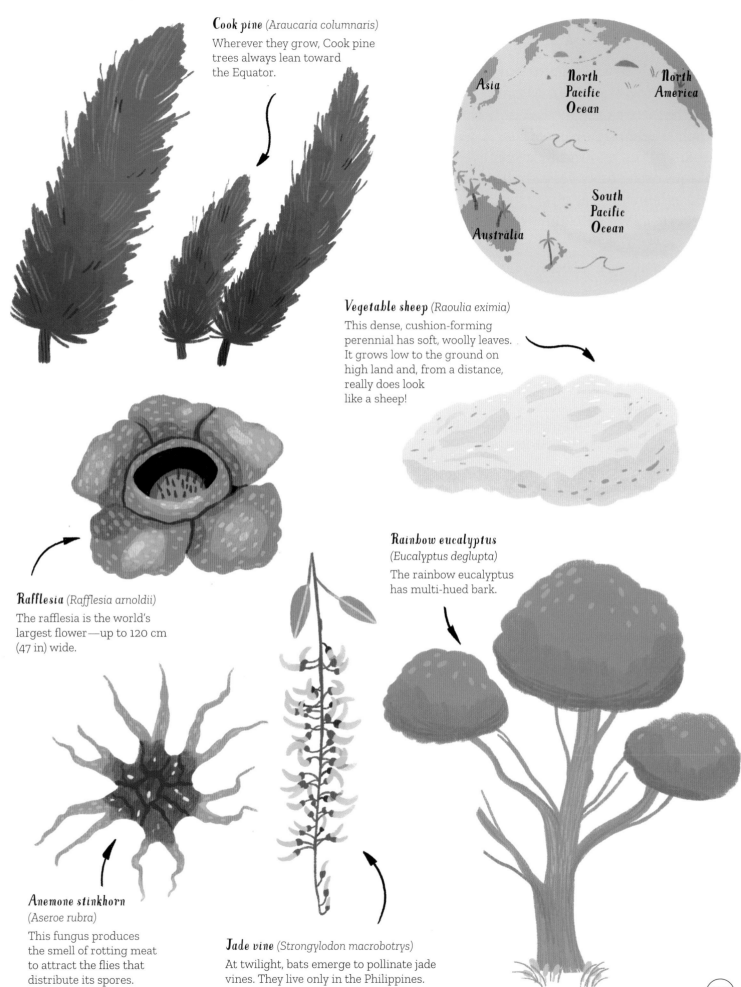

Cook pine (*Araucaria columnaris*)
Wherever they grow, Cook pine trees always lean toward the Equator.

Asia

North Pacific Ocean

North America

South Pacific Ocean

Australia

Vegetable sheep (*Raoulia eximia*)
This dense, cushion-forming perennial has soft, woolly leaves. It grows low to the ground on high land and, from a distance, really does look like a sheep!

Rainbow eucalyptus
(*Eucalyptus deglupta*)
The rainbow eucalyptus has multi-hued bark.

Rafflesia (*Rafflesia arnoldii*)
The rafflesia is the world's largest flower—up to 120 cm (47 in) wide.

Anemone stinkhorn
(*Aseroe rubra*)
This fungus produces the smell of rotting meat to attract the flies that distribute its spores.

Jade vine (*Strongylodon macrobotrys*)
At twilight, bats emerge to pollinate jade vines. They live only in the Philippines.

THE ARCTIC

The Arctic is a beautiful but challenging habitat. Deep snow, strong winds, and extremely low temperatures mean that only those plants with special adaptations can thrive. Permafrost keeps much of the ground frozen all year so Arctic plants often have very shallow roots that spread out sideways to anchor them instead of growing directly down into the ground.

To make the best use of the available sunshine, many species have dark green leaves that absorb more light. During the short summer, the areas north of the Arctic circle and south of the Antarctic circle experience "midnight Sun"—24 hours of light each day. In the winter, the Sun never rises. This is the "polar night."

Some plants reproduce quickly and die when the winter returns. Others take life more slowly, growing a few millimeters each year. Some cushion plants may be only 15 cm (6 in) wide but can be 250 years old.

Arctic lupine
(Lupinus arcticus)
Arctic lupine seeds that are 10,000 years old were found frozen in a lemming burrow. Once thawed, they started to germinate.

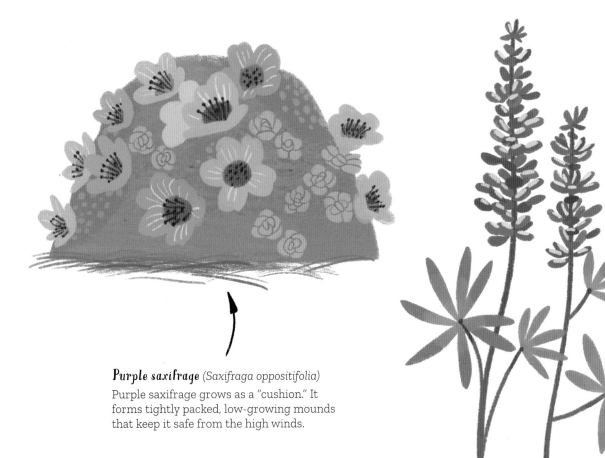

Purple saxifrage *(Saxifraga oppositifolia)*
Purple saxifrage grows as a "cushion." It forms tightly packed, low-growing mounds that keep it safe from the high winds.

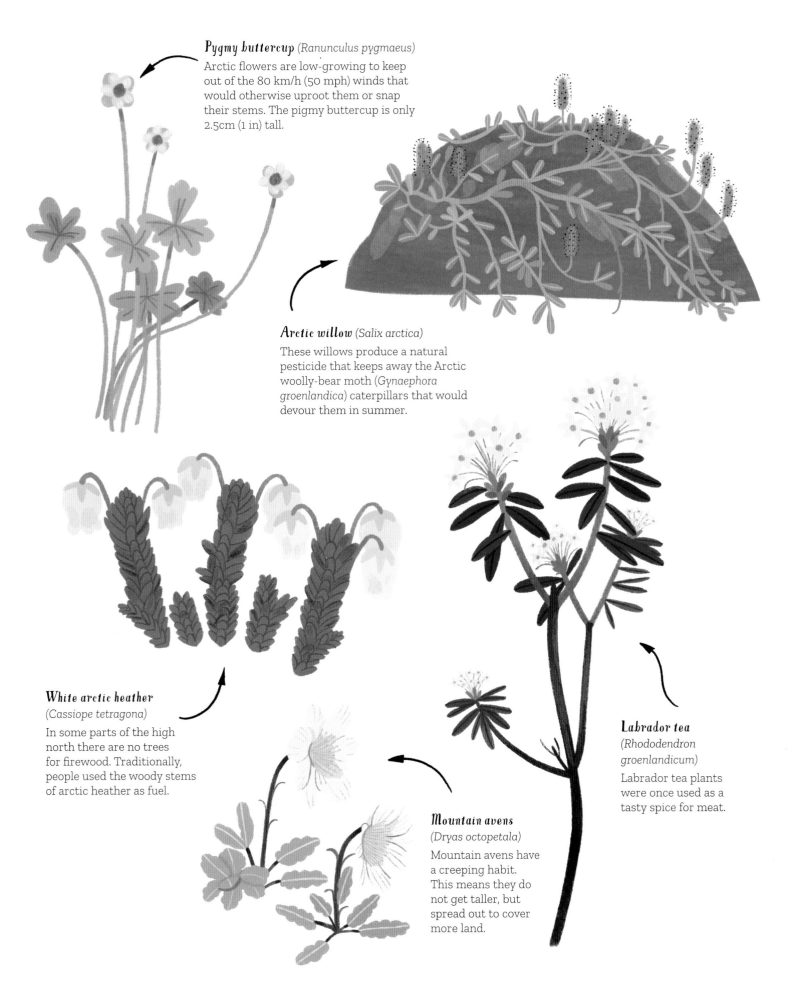

Pygmy buttercup *(Ranunculus pygmaeus)*
Arctic flowers are low-growing to keep out of the 80 km/h (50 mph) winds that would otherwise uproot them or snap their stems. The pigmy buttercup is only 2.5cm (1 in) tall.

Arctic willow *(Salix arctica)*
These willows produce a natural pesticide that keeps away the Arctic woolly-bear moth *(Gynaephora groenlandica)* caterpillars that would devour them in summer.

White arctic heather
(Cassiope tetragona)
In some parts of the high north there are no trees for firewood. Traditionally, people used the woody stems of arctic heather as fuel.

Mountain avens
(Dryas octopetala)
Mountain avens have a creeping habit. This means they do not get taller, but spread out to cover more land.

Labrador tea
(Rhododendron groenlandicum)
Labrador tea plants were once used as a tasty spice for meat.

THE ANTARCTIC

The Antarctic is the coldest, driest, and least inhabited of all the world's continents. It is also the most challenging habitat for any living species to survive—plants or animals. There is little soil and land is buried beneath a massive layer of ice.

Little lives on the Antarctic mainland. More species can be found on the nearby sub-Antarctic islands. But plants are adaptable, and when they cannot survive on land, the sea offers an alternative. The oceans are home to phytoplankton—hundreds of billions of microscopic floating plants of countless species. They drift around the Antarctic using sunlight to photosynthesize and release oxygen. Approximately 75 percent of the Earth's oxygen is produced by these tiny plants—oxygen that is needed by every living creature. Phytoplankton are the smallest and most important species in this book. Without them, life as we know it would not be possible on Earth.

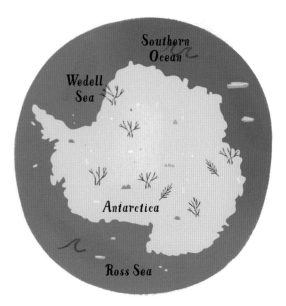

Fossil evidence
The land at the Antarctic was once a tropical rain forest. We know this because beneath the snow are fossils of ancient tree ferns.

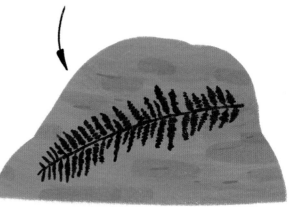

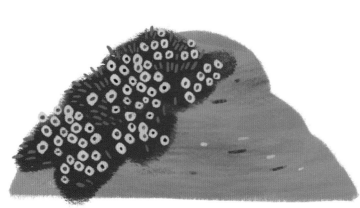

Antarctic pearlwort
(*Colobanthus quitensis*)

Pearlwort is one of only two flowering plants that survive on the main Antarctic landmass. It grows close to the coast, where snow sometimes melts in summer.

Crustose lichen
(*Lecanora conizaeoides*)

Crustose lichens are impossible to remove because they bond so tightly to the rocks on which they grow.

Life-giving phytoplankton

Much of the oxygen in your lungs right now is produced by these tiny marine plants as they drift around the Antarctic.

Antarctic hair grass
(Deschampsia antarctica)

Hair grass grows farther south than any other flowering plant.

Mountain pincushion
(Dicranoweisia crispula)

The mountain pincushion is a moss that grows in both the Arctic and the Antarctic.

Glacier mice

The size of tennis balls, mysterious glacier mice are small colonies of mosses that move slowly, in herds, across the ice. Very little is known about how or why they move.

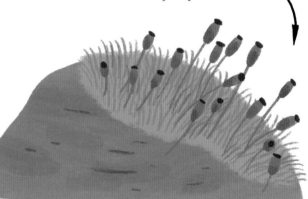

Antarctic moss
(Schistidium antarctica)

Antarctic moss grows in soft, yellowish green, dome-shaped clumps that sometimes cover large areas of rock.

PLANTS UNDER THREAT

Extinction is a natural process. New species evolve and others vanish, but threats to plant life are occurring at a different pace today. It is estimated that about 40 percent of all species are at risk of extinction. We are changing the planet so quickly that ecosystems and environments have no time to evolve.

Habitat destruction and pollution endanger plant life around the world. When peatlands are drained, oceans are polluted, or when complex ancient forests are cut down, they cannot be replaced. The ecosystems they are part of are broken. This damages life above ground, underwater, and also inside the soil, where plant roots exchange nutrients and information with others.

DEFORESTATION

Forests are being destroyed to develop land for grazing, farming, and logging. In 100 years, there may be no rain forests left.

HABITAT DEGRADATION

Rich, biodiverse ecosystems are being damaged by soil erosion and land contamination.

INVASIVE SPECIES

When plants are taken from one habitat to another, they can squeeze out native plants. They can also hybridize with native species and overwhelm them.

POLLUTION

Pollution damages fragile ecosystems and plant habitats.

OVEREXPLOITATION

The products of land, waters, and forests are being taken faster than they can reproduce.

CLIMATE CHANGE—THE BIGGEST THREAT OF ALL

Life on Earth would be impossible without the Sun. It provides the heat and light that allows plants and animals to survive. But they all need a "habitable zone"—an environment that is not too hot and not too cold, but just right.

Humans produce excess greenhouse gases, such as carbon dioxide and methane. These gases form a layer over the atmosphere that acts like a blanket and stops heat from escaping. This means the planet becomes warmer. Rising temperatures melt the polar ice, change the weather, and alter most of the world's habitats—threatening the survival of all life.

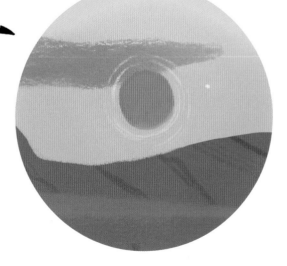

PLANTS AND PEOPLE

Plants support life. They feed the world with grains, fruits, and vegetables. They give us medicines, clothing, fuel, and materials for building. Most importantly, they also give us life-giving oxygen.

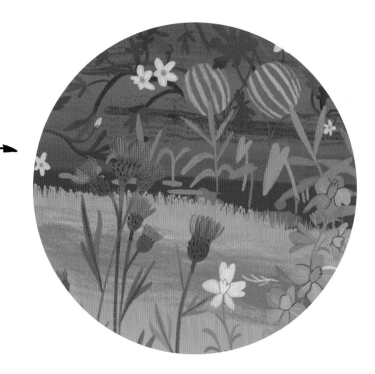

FARMING

The earliest people were nomadic and gathered food from the wild. The first farming began in the "Fertile Crescent" in the Middle East around 12,000 years ago. People learned to sow, harvest, and store crops and to domesticate animals. Over time, they also selectively bred crops that would produce better yields and have greater disease resistance. Farming became more intensive. Today, half of the global population relies on rice, maize, and wheat. It is estimated that 15 species of plants provide 90 percent of all calories. We also rely on plants to feed livestock.

TREASURE CHEST

We could not live without plants. More than 50,000 plants provide medicines. Trees provide us with timber for buildings and furniture. They give us paper. Cotton, hemp, and bamboo provide fabrics for clothing. Plants can be transformed into biofuels and cosmetics. They also provide oils.

NATURE'S SPICE CABINET

Herbs and spices help preserve our food and add taste.

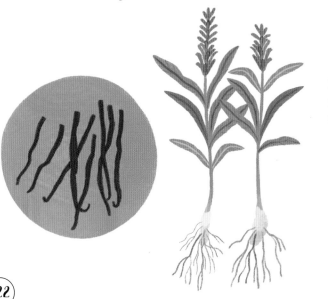

WELL-BEING

Spending time in green spaces improves our concentration and reduces stress. In Japan, this is called *shinrin-yoku* or "forest bathing." Whether we explore a city park or a hike into the forest, time spent among plants is healing. The same can be said of growing things. Gardens, window boxes, and houseplants can benefit our minds and our bodies.

INVESTING IN THE FUTURE

To help maintain plant biodiversity, scientists all around the world have created seed banks. The most varied is the Svalbard Global Seed Vault, which is built into an icy mountain in Norway. Established in 2008, today it holds about 1 million seeds. This is one of the ways in which we protect plant life for future generations.

PLANTS TO THE RESCUE

Plants help us in the fight against global warming. Forests on land and in the sea help store carbon and slow climate change. By protecting the land, waters, and air, we should be able to create sustainable crop solutions to global hunger and energy needs.

HOW TO HELP PLANTS AND THE PLANET

Plant life is essential to the planet and it faces many threats. Habitat loss, deforestation, overgrazing, water pollution, and climate change all pose challenges. What can we do to help?

CONNECT WITH OTHERS

Find conservation organizations or rescue hubs working in your area and volunteer.

Use social media to share the things you care about. There are many excellent young environmental campaigners active online.

LEARN, LEARN, LEARN!

The more we know about the natural world, the better we can care for it.

- Be curious! Read, watch, listen, and learn about plants and their habitats.

- Learn about the oceans and the huge variety of life they contain.

- Learn about the threats we and our planet face and how to help.

- Talk about what you are learning—with family, friends, and your wider community.

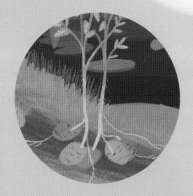

GROW!

Get hands on and grow something! Even if you only have a space as small as a windowsill, you can experiment with growing your own food—herbs, cress, radishes, or pea shoots are delicious choices.

GREAT OAKS GROW FROM LITTLE ACORNS

Remember—no action is too small! If we each take tiny steps to protect the planet, we can go far together.

WHEN YOU ARE HIKING

- Stay on trails or paths so young plants stay safe and do not get trampled.

- Do not light fires.

- Leave gates open or closed as you found them and obey any signs and local laws.

CONNECT WITH NATURE EVERY DAY

- Spend as much time as you can outside exploring. Not just in the sunshine, but in the rain and the wind, too.

- Take photographs of plants and wild places that you like; draw or write about them.

- Make a collection of finds from your walks; seeds, leaves, and interesting pieces of bark are all great discoveries. Photograph the finds and share them with your friends.

- Keep a nature diary.

WAYS TO HELP SAVE TREES

- Do not waste paper.
- Borrow, share, and donate books.
- Plant a tree if you can!

REUSE, RECYCLE, AND TRY NOT TO WASTE ANYTHING!

Changes in the climate are dangerous for the planet. We can all play a role in helping to stop global warming:

- Turn off lights when not using them.

- Try not to buy things you do not need.

- Park the car! If you can walk or cycle to school or to see a friend safely, do!

- Try not to leave taps running.

- Think about what you eat and try to make environmentally sustainable choices. Eat more locally produced vegetables, fruits, and beans.

- Avoid single-use plastics.

GLOSSARY

Agriculture   Farming plants and raising animals for human use.

Algae   Plant-like organisms that usually live in water.

Bark   Outer layer of roots, trunks, and branches of trees and shrubs.

Biodiversity   The variety of species living in one area.

Biome   Large community of plants and animals living in a major habitat.

Bonsai   A tree or shrub kept in miniature form by pruning.

Bract   A type of leaf, sometimes brightly toned. May attract pollinators.

Bulb   Underground onion-like structure that stores food for a plant during its dormant period.

Chlorophyll   A green pigment used by plant cells to gather energy from the Sun.

Cloning   Asexual plant reproduction.

Conifer   Cone-bearing evergreen tree or shrub with needle-like leaves.

Deciduous   A plant that sheds leaves each year.

Desert   A place where little rain falls.

Dormant   An inactive state in which plants remain alive but do not grow.

Ecosystem   Community of animals and plants and their shared environment.

Epiphyte   A plant that grows on another plant without taking nutrients from it.

Evergreen   A plant that keeps its leaves all year.

Fertilization   Combining of a male pollen cell and a female egg.

Flower   Part of the reproductive structure of some plants. Within their petals are the parts that produce pollen and seeds.

Freshwater   Rivers or lakes with a low concentrations of salts.

Fungus   Microorganisms that live alongside plants but are more closely related to animals.

Germination   The process by which seeds begin to grow.

Harvest   The process of gathering crops when ripe.

Herbaceous   Plants without woody stems that die back after fruiting.

Lichen	An organism made of both fungi and algae working together.
Mycelium	Thread-like part of a fungus, usually underground or inside another material.
Nectar	A sugary fluid produced by plants to attract pollinators.
Nutrients	Minerals used by a plant to enable growth.
Perennial	Plants that live for more than two years.
Petals	Brightly hued parts of a flower that attract pollinators.
Photosynthesis	How a green plant uses energy from the Sun, water from soil, and carbon dioxide from air to create food for itself.
Phytoplankton	Tiny marine plants that produce oxygen.
Plant	A living organism that produces its own food by photosynthesis.
Pollen	Tiny grains that contain male reproductive cells.
Pollination	The transfer of male pollen grains to the female parts of a flower. This fertilizes eggs and produces seed.
Pollinator	An animal that moves pollen from flower to flower.
Rain forest	Woodlands that receive more than 200 cm (80 in) of rain each year.
Saltwater	Water containing high amounts of salts, such as the oceans.
Sap	The juices in plants.
Seed	Reproductive structure containing the embryo of the plant, nutrients, and a seed covering.
Seed dispersal	Ways in which seeds are carried from the parent plant to a new place.
Shrub	Woody, multi-stemmed bush.
Spore	Tiny reproductive structure found in non-flowering plants such as ferns.
Succulent	A plant, such as a cactus, that stores water in thickened leaves or stems.
Tree	A tall, woody plant with a trunk and branches.
Tuber	The thick underground stem or root that some plants use to store nutrients.
Vine	A plant that climbs or trails over the ground and supports itself by tendrils or by twining through other structures.

INDEX